HRJC

D0847798

Folktales from the Japanese Countryside

World Folklore Advisory Board

Folktales from the Japanese Countryside

As told by Hiroko Fujita

Edited by Fran Stallings
with Harold Wright and Miki Sakurai

World Folklore Series

LIBRARIES
UNLIMITED
A Member of the Greenwood Publishing Group

Westport, Connecticut • London

Library of Congress Cataloging-in-Publication Data

Fujita, Hiroko, 1937-
  Folktales from the Japanese countryside / as told by Hiroko Fujita ;
  edited by Fran Stallings with Harold Wright and Miki Sakurai.
    p. cm. — (World folklore series)
  Includes bibliographical references and index.
  ISBN-13: 978-1-59158-488-9 (alk. paper)
  1. Tales—Japan. 2. Folklore—Japan. I. Stallings, Fran.
  II. Wright, Harold, 1931- III. Sakurai, Miki, 1933- IV. Title.
  GR340.F826 2008
  398.20952—dc22   2007017727

British Library Cataloguing in Publication Data is available.

Library of Congress Catalog Card Number: 2007017727
ISBN-13: 978-1-59158-488-9

First published in 2008

Libraries Unlimited, 88 Post Road West, Westport, CT 06881
A Member of the Greenwood Publishing Group, Inc.
www.lu.com

Printed in the United States of America

The paper used in this book complies with the
Permanent Paper Standard issued by the National
Information Standards Organization (Z39.48–1984).

10   9   8   7   6   5   4   3   2   1

Cover illustration by Kyoko Kobayashi, "Tanabata: Star Festival" (see "The Home of the Bush
Warbler").

The publisher has done its best to make sure the instructions and/or recipes in this book are correct. However, users should apply judgment and experience when preparing recipes, especially
parents and teachers working with young people. The publisher accepts no responsibility for the
outcome of any recipe included in this volume.

*This book is dedicated to Takeda Kuni and Toshiko Endo,
traditional country folktellers who preserved the tales they had
heard as children and passed them along to Hiroko Fujita.*

*It is also dedicated to the many listeners of all ages on both sides
of the Pacific Ocean who loved hearing Hiroko Fujita's tales and
begged for more.*

CONTENTS

Part 3: Stories of Priests and Apprentices

Part 4: Stories of Strange Happenings

Part 5: Stories of Yamanbas

Part 6: Stories of Supernatural Creatures

Part 7: Food, Games, and Crafts

ACKNOWLEDGMENTS

I met Hiroko Fujita in Japan in 1993. In 1995 we began annual spring tours of America to share her lively Japanese tales with American listeners of all ages, and in autumn 1997 she began bringing me to Japan to tell American stories. (I took the color photos in this book during our 1999 and 2001 tours of Japan.) While we traveled, Mrs. Fujita would often tell me a tale whenever an incident or sight reminded her of one. I couldn't write them down while driving, so I'm very grateful that her followers, "The Young Yamanbas," have preserved her stories.

The Young Yamanbas recorded, transcribed, and privately printed Hiroko Fujita's colloquial Japanese storytelling in six volumes, titled *Katare Yamanba* (*Speak, Mountain-woman!*). The English retellings in this book are based on translations by Makiko Ishibashi, Nobumichi and Yoko Iwasa, Mitsuko Harada, and Satomi Obata. This book would not have been possible without their work. But the rough English translations languished in my computer for years. I am very grateful to Libraries Unlimited for giving us the chance at last to share them with story-lovers everywhere.

The cover and interior illustrations are by one of The Young Yamanbas, Kyoko Kobayashi. Translator Makiko Ishibashi helped in many ways, especially by interpreting and negotiating between me and all the talented Japanese people.

Harold Wright, emeritus professor of Japanese at Antioch University, contributed "A Brief History of Japan." In addition, he and his wife Jonatha scrupulously reviewed the story texts, advising on details of culture and translation. Miki Sakurai, founder and president of the Japanese Storytellers Association, contributed the essay "Storytelling in Japan." We thank them for their generous help.

The recipes, provided by Michiyo McMillan and Yumie Farringer, were tested by Virgil, Helen, and Laura Reese and Ben Stallings. Nancy Lenhart tested the Kappa toy directions. Michiyo McMillan interpreted some tricky words and directions and helped me work on my Japanese. Last but hardly least, we appreciate our families, who have steadfastly encouraged us in our trans-Pacific projects.

Thanks to the help and advice of all these people and our editors at Libraries Unlimited, we hope that this book will be as useful and delightful as the ancient folktales themselves.

Fran Stallings

A BRIEF HISTORY OF JAPAN

Harold Wright, emeritus professor of Japanese, Antioch College

When Americans picture Japan, we often think of such things as samurai warriors, geisha, Zen Buddhism, flower arrangements, wood-block prints, the tea ceremony, Kabuki and Noh theater, haiku poetry, and sushi . . . but none of these things existed when the folktales we enjoy today were first told around warming fires in farmhouses. Much of what we think of as Japanese culture developed as late as the Tokugawa Period (1600–1868), when Japan was almost totally closed to the Western world.

The word "Japan" is close in pronunciation to what the Chinese called their neighbor, and it is this term that was brought back to Europe by the earliest travelers from the West. The Japanese people themselves call it *Nihon* (sun origin). The language they speak is officially known as *nihongo*, a rather unique language in the human family of tongues, not related to the Chinese language at all.

We believe that in prehistoric times, when the Japanese Sea was merely a lake, people crossed over from the Asian mainland in search of game. Later, other people sailed in boats from China and Korea, or by following the warm currents of the sea from Southeast Asia. They brought myths, legends, pottery skills, and later, metalworking skills from the mainland. The unique Japanese language and culture developed from this rich mixture of cultures of ancient Asia through centuries of isolation and peace.

Japan is a long, narrow country that lies just over 100 miles from the tip of Korea and roughly 500 miles over open sea from China. It was distant enough from the Asian mainland to avoid being conquered (at least until defeated in World War II) but close enough to welcome a constant flow of the high culture of China: a writing system, art, ideas of government, city planning, architecture, medicine, ritualized tea drinking, and Confucian philosophy, as well as the Indian religion of Buddhism.

If a map of Japan were placed over a map of the United States, we would see that its islands stretch from Maine to Florida. Japan's climate ranges from snowbound winters in the north to semitropics in the south. The ancient capital of Kyoto has hot, humid summers much like Atlanta, Georgia. Japan is not really the small, cramped country we often hear about in the news. Television usually shows crowded conditions in the present capital city Tokyo or packed express trains rushing to Osaka and beyond. Over 80 percent of the land in

Japan, however, is uninhabited mountains. It is a wonderful land for religious pilgrims, who still worship the mountain deities or visit hidden Buddhist temples on the slopes of snow-covered peaks. The mountains are popular also with generations of backpackers and skiers. Hiking is a favorite sport among senior citizens today. Perhaps because of such healthy activities and a nutritious diet, the Japanese are among the longest-lived people on Earth.

Fresh and dried fish, shellfish, and even seaweed have always been important in the Japanese diet, along with many kinds of vegetables. Rice, however, has always been the most important staple crop. Farmers also raised wheat, barley, millet, and buckwheat, on which they survived in years when all of their rice crop went to pay their land tax. Meat eating was not popular until modern times because of Buddhist taboos against taking life. But now hamburgers are as popular as they are anywhere in the world. Ice cream is replacing the traditional dessert of shaved ice with sweet syrup.

The indigenous religion, Shinto (the way of the gods), is the spiritual force behind many of the yearly festivals, which fascinate visitors to Japan. Even after Buddhism became the national religion in the eighth century, Shinto was not replaced but has continued as a parallel faith; most Japanese participate in both Shinto and Buddhist cultural activities. Some people add rituals of other religions as well. Christmas, Halloween, and Christian-style weddings have become popular.

In Shinto, the dead are sometimes believed to be still alive in spirit form and are feared or worshiped. Shinto deities in Japan include awe-inspiring natural phenomena such as unusually shaped rocks; mountains such as the famed Mt. Fuji; waterfalls; ancient trees; and the souls of important historical figures, including all the emperors and empresses. The imperial family of Japan is the oldest continuing dynasty on Earth. Emperor Akihito is believed to be the 125th ruler in a long line of men and some women who reach back to the "age of the gods" and even to Amaterasu Omikami, the sun goddess herself. Mythology tells us it was she who sent down a member of her own family, the Emperor Jimmu, in 660 BCE to rule the earth as the first emperor. Although archeology and solid history have given us a different picture of ancient Japan, the imperial line does go back for at least 1,300 years. Now the emperor is no longer considered sacred but, like the royal family of the British Isles, he and his family serve as symbols of the country and are the subjects of many stories and photographs in the news.

Japan is now a democracy, with a prime minister and a parliament, known as the Diet. Young men and women look forward to turning twenty, at which age they become legal adults and can vote. Education is extremely important in Japan, and the country has one of the highest literacy rates in the world.

Historical Highlights

The Ancient Period to 794

Japanese written history extends back nearly 1,300 years. Japan's oldest books contain myths, legends, and folktales, as well as bits of real history. Due to the high literacy rate of the Japanese, there has always been an intermingling of written and oral literatures. Folktales have been written down since the eighth century. An oral story could be written down, then read or told aloud over and over again until it developed into a somewhat changed oral tale in another hamlet, in a mountain valley, or in a fishing village by the sea.

The ancient origin myths of the Japanese were first recorded using a writing system borrowed from visiting Chinese or Koreans. The oldest extant book is the *Kojiki* (*Record of Ancient Matters*), dating from 712 CE. This first attempt to record Japanese oral stories in Chinese characters was not an easy task because the two languages are linguistically so different. The second oldest book, *Nihon Shoki* (*Chronicles of Japan,* also called *Nihongi*), appeared in 720. Both these books tell the story of Izanagi and Izanami, the father and mother of the land. Both books also tell the story of Amaterasu Omikami, the sun goddess, and her brother Susanoo Omikami, the sea or storm god, and their adventures and descendants. The stories of the sun goddess closing herself up in a cave and casting the world into darkness, and of Susanoo slaying a huge serpent to save a young woman, are still told in Japan. The story of Emperor Jimmu arriving on Earth to rule the land is told as a part of the origin myth of Japan. Similar to our own Bible stories, these tales are known by nearly all Japanese. There are even *manga* (comic book) versions.

Nara, the first permanent capital of Japan, was founded in the year 710, during the ancient period. With Buddhism becoming a state religion, a famed Great Buddha was built in Nara and all the wonderful Buddhist tales from India and China entered the land. Both written and told versions were known throughout the country. The first imperial collection of poetry, the *Manyoshu* (*Collection of Ten-thousand Leaves*), containing over 5,000 ancient poems, was read widely in aristocratic circles. Some of the poems were based on existing folktales such as the story of *Urashima Taro,* the fisherman who lived for 300 years in the kingdom under the sea.

Heian Period (794–1185)

In 794 the capital of Japan was moved to Kyoto, where it remained for over a thousand years. In the Heian period, Kyoto was the center of a flowering of Japanese aristocratic culture. It was a glorious period for the production of art and literature. By this time a simple phonetic syllabic script had been developed to permit people to write down quickly anything they could say. Oral tales or new literary works could now be recorded easily. Both men and women wrote poems, especially in the thirty-one-syllable form called *tanka*, and prose, particularly narrative fiction and diaries.

Taketori Monogatari (*Tale of the Bamboo Cutter*), the "parent" of all tales, was finally written down. The rich narrative style of this story, which tells of an old man finding a beautiful, tiny girl in a stalk of bamboo, had much influence on later written literature, such as the *Genji Monogatari* (*The Tale of Genji*) by Lady Murasaki Shikibu. Considered the world's first realistic novel, *Genji* was written down around a thousand years ago. The exact dates are not known, but it must have taken years to write this book, which can be over a thousand pages in translation. It contains many stories and subplots, mostly about life in the ancient court at Kyoto.

Konjaku Monogatari (*Tales of Long Ago*) contains over 1,200 tales from India, China, and Japan. Collected in the eleventh century, it is considered the first, if not the most important, collection of many of the Japanese folktales we now enjoy. Not all of the stories have yet appeared in English translation.

Kamakura Period (1185–1333)

After a series of civil wars that brought about the decline of the aristocracy in Kyoto and the rise of the samurai warriors as the rulers of Japan, the Shogun (Generalissimo) ruled from Kamakura. However, the imperial capital of Japan, with the emperor and family, remained in Kyoto.

Heike Monogatari (*The Tale of the Heike*) is the best known of the "war tales," which describe the civil wars at the end of the Heian period. Moving tales of heroism are told within the framework of a Buddhist message about the futility of worldly matters. *The Tale of Heike* contains many shorter legends and subplots. Many of the stories lived on to become other works of literature, including both aristocratic Noh plays and the later popular dramatic pieces of the Kabuki stage.

Uji Shui Monogatari (*Tales from the Uji Collection*) is a major collection of 195 folktales from the early thirteenth century. A number of well-known Japanese fairy tales, such as "The Grateful Sparrow," appear in this work.

Muromachi-Momoyama (1333–1600)

Increasing civil war and political conflict plagued Japan for several centuries. Muromachi and Momoyama were places in or near Kyoto where the samurai held seats of power. At one point there were two emperors and two courts. One remained in Kyoto, while the other was in the Yoshino mountains south of the city. This is also the period when Noh theater and comic Kyogen plays developed.

There was much contact with China during these times. The Zen form of Buddhism came to Japan from the mainland, and with it all Zen-influenced arts like flower arrangement, the tea ceremony, landscape painting, and gardening. In the early 1500s the Portuguese and the Spanish also came to Japan, bringing crosses and guns.

Collections of *Otogizoshi* (shorter prose stories, often translated as "nursery tales") began to appear. Many of these stories dealt with the lives and loves of the aristocrats as well as Buddhist tales. A well-known Buddhist tale is *Sannin Hoshi* ("The Three Priests"), in which fate brings together in peace both the lover and the killer of a young woman, to become priests in the same monastery. However, there also appeared stories that would appeal to the children of samurai and families of a new rising merchant class. *Issun Boshi* ("Little One Inch") was printed at this time.

Gikeiki (*Life of Minamoto Yoshitsune*) is the major collection of legends of the famed samurai of the twelfth century. It is said that this renowned warrior learned magical powers and amazing swordsmanship from the *Tengu,* mythological beings living in the mountains north of Kyoto. This collection records legends that are still told in mountain communities all over Japan.

Tokugawa or Edo Period (1600–1868)

Tokugawa Ieyasu ruled as Shogun from the city of Edo (now known as Tokyo). Due to fear of external influences and control, Japan's borders were closed to the outside world. Portuguese and Spanish Christians faced expulsion or death. No Japanese were permitted to go abroad. No foreigners were allowed to be in Japan except the Englishman Will Adams, who became an advisor to the Shogun, and the protestant Dutch, who were required to restrict themselves to trading in nonreligious products and living on a man-made island off the coast of Nagasaki in the south.

Inside the closed borders of Japan, however, a new culture flourished for the merchants and artisans in the large cities of Edo (Tokyo), Osaka, and Kyoto. Kabuki was the new theater. Cheaply printed novels, chapbooks of stories, and wood-block prints appeared everywhere. Stories were still told orally in rural communities all over the country, but due to the high literacy rate of all classes and the availably of cheap paperbacks, there was a very close relationship between the written and spoken forms. Tales of the bizarre and the supernatural, and especially legends of ghosts, were very popular.

Japanese society was rigidly divided at this time into four classes. The samurai were at the top because they maintained the relatively peaceful police state. The farmers came second because they produced rice, the currency of the land. Third were the artisans because they produced useful products like houses, boats, paper, and all the things needed for daily life. Last came the merchants, who were not respected at all because they just bought and sold things. However, it was the merchants who took control of the wealth of the land and moved the country from a rice standard to the gold standard economy of modern Japan. The *choja*, often mentioned in folktales, was not an official class, but rather anyone fortunate enough to have wealth. Like Jack in our own folk tradition in the United States, the choja could become rich through pure luck.

Modern Period: 1868 to the Present

Modern Japan's history is often divided into eras named for its emperors. Remember that Japan has the oldest existing dynasty in the world. The present Hesei emperor is believed to be the 125th in a long line that extends back into the prehistoric past.

Most U.S. history books tell the story of Commodore Perry going to Japan in the 1850s with his "Black Ships" to open up that closed country. Japan was ready to open, and did so fully in 1868 when the Meiji emperor (1868–1912) moved the capital from Kyoto to Edo and changed the name of that samurai city from Edo to Tokyo (Eastern Capital). Emperor Meiji led Japan into the modern world. He started wearing Western clothes, as did his wife, Empress Shoken.

The four classes of society were abolished and the samurai gave up the right to carry swords. The former warriors were also ordered to get Western-style haircuts. Some carried walking sticks in the Western fashion and wore leather shoes. Women were attracted to the long gowns and large hats of the Victorian West. Some carried parasols to protect their delicate skin from the sun. People even started eating beef! The Japanese leaned how to build a modern army from the Prussians, a navy from the English, a new postal system from the French, and railroads from the Americans. Japan won two wars, first against the Chinese in 1895, then against the Russians in 1905.

The Taisho emperor (1912–1926) ruled from Tokyo while "jazz age" popular culture swept the world after World War I. It was the age of the modern novel, modern poetry and art, and formation of a contemporary theater. Men and women, even aristocrats, enjoyed dancing in public. Popular storytelling theaters operated all over the country in cities, allowing people to laugh loudly at the comic *rakugo* (male stage storytellers for adults). Movies were becoming popular as well. Stories were still told orally in rural communities throughout the land.

The Showa emperor (1926–1989) is best known in the West by his given name of Hirohito—which out of respect was not used in Japan. As he ruled from his secluded palace in Tokyo, Japan became more and more a military state, expanding into other areas of Asia. The bombing of Pearl Harbor in Hawaii in 1941 brought the United States into World War II, which ended with the atomic bombing of Hiroshima and Nagasaki. Older Japanese people still remember the suffering they experienced during the war years, especially the bombing of their cities. In 1945 the Showa emperor denounced his divinity and fully embraced the democratic modernization of his country. Japan became one of the major, economically strong democracies of the world.

In 1948 the internationally renowned folklorist Yanagita Kunio published his important *Nihon mukashibanashi meii* (*Guide to the Japanese Folk Tale*). In this work he collected and categorized oral stories from all over Japan. This work is now available to storytellers and researchers everywhere through Fanny Hagin Mayer's translation as *The Yanagita Kunio Guide to the Japanese Folk Tale* (1986).

The Showa period also brought about an innovative type of storytelling, *kamishibai* (literally "paper drama"). As far back as the twelfth century, Buddhist priests and nuns had used picture scrolls to help convey stories with moral lessons to their congregations. But starting in the 1920s, storytellers rode bicycles, with stagelike boxes of pictures attached to the carrying rack, through villages and even cities to tell stories to children. To support themselves, they usually sold candy to the children before finishing their traditional folktales. As they told in animated gestures they dramatically flashed illustrations, one after another, before the excited children. The practice began to fade with the introduction of television in the 1950s. Some of the kamishibai artists went on to become animation illustrators for the new medium.

Heisei Emperor Akihito (1989 to the present) broke tradition by marrying outside the aristocratic families. He met Miss Michiko Shoda playing tennis, and like many young people today they even went on dates. Married on April 10, 1959, they have two sons and a daughter.

Storytelling is still alive in Japan. Kamishibai and picture books of traditional stories are popular in schools and libraries. Storytellers and story readers are everywhere in Japan. There was even a popular television program that showed animated versions of the ancient stories. Many young people today learned the old stories from that series. Many tellers and researchers are turning to the old tales recorded in ancient books; others are listening to the stories of older generations. Libraries and cultural centers are collecting stories of the elders. But there is still the interplay of the oral tradition and the written text that has played such an important part in Japanese folktale history. Now video cameras, tape recorders, and CD players are important tools in the collecting of stories. Novelists, film directors, and animation artists such as Academy Award winner Hayao Miyazaki are returning to Japanese myth, legend, and folk themes for their contemporary work. Shinto shrines and Buddhist temples now sell comic book versions of their sacred stories. Tales over a thousand years old are still told today, and those stories continue to evolve and live on.

STORYTELLING IN JAPAN

Miki Sakurai, president, The Japan Storytellers Association

Oral Tradition in Japanese Literature

Early in the eighth century, two books of Japanese mythology that included narratives by storytellers were written in Japan. *Kojiki* (*The Records of Ancient Matters*) (712 CE) is the oldest book based on oral tradition in Japan. *Nihonshoki* (720 CE) was written by historians of the Yamato court to establish Japanese history as fact.

Kojiki was recorded almost 1,300 years ago. It shows what narratives were told before the introduction of writing to Japan. Through the stories in *Kojiki* we can imagine the original styles of the oral narratives. There are world creation myths, tales of the birth of gods and goddesses, the pantheon's love and marriage stories, accounts of the power struggles among the clans and in imperial families, and adventures of heroes. Many motifs in Japanese folktales can be found in *Kojiki,* and we recognize original versions of Japanese folktales as told before the seventh century.

In the medieval period, from the ninth to the thirteenth centuries, members of the emperor's court wrote down many stories. In some books there are stories that were also told in towns and villages at that time. Some of them start with the Japanese version of "Once upon a time . . ." .

The professional storytellers appeared in the medieval period. They told stories while playing musical instruments in town streets, and many of them were blind. *Goze* (blind female tellers who traveled in small troupes) told family tragedy or revenge stories while striking the hand drum. Other professional storytellers were *biwa-hoshi* (blind male tellers traveling solo), who told the epic of the Heike clan while playing the *biwa*, a stringed instrument.

Storytelling as public entertainment relating to Buddhism also arose in medieval times. Stories of *Sekkyobushi* were generally told in the towns. These were stories of revenge, parent and child separations, and so on, in which people were saved from tragic situations by Buddhism. Musical instruments were used as accompaniment. Many of the *Sekkyobushi* stories entered the repertoires of the theater arts, which began to emerge at the end of the Middle Ages. Today we can still enjoy the same stories that were told by medieval professional artists.

Stories were handed down orally generation after generation in villages in every part of Japan until the twentieth century. People handed down folk narrative by word of mouth.

Japanese Folktales in Modern Times

In 1908 Dr. Kunio Yanagita started the collection and academic study of Japanese folk narratives. Many scholars subsequently continued his work researching folktales. In the 1950s Dr. Yanagita's apprentice, Dr. Keigo Seki, classified Japanese folktales based on *The Types of the Folktale* by Aarne and Thompson.

Dr. Yanagita assumed that animal tales were the oldest stories in Japan as well as in other cultures. Some animal tales were probably told about 10,000 years ago. Scholars think they were carried from Siberia to Japan.

"The Ordinary Tales" had been told here and there in the Japanese countryside since the Middle Ages. Typical tales were "Peach Boy," "Inch Boy," and "The Monkey and the Crab." Others were "Obtains the Treasure," "Animal Wives," "The Three Brothers," "The Three Sisters," and stepchild stories. These folktales contain motifs common to Japan and other countries.

After the Pacific War (World War II), Japanese folktales were rediscovered as part of an art culture movement featuring plays based on folktales. "The folktale boom" was not only in theaters but also in publishing. At that time traditional storytellers who had grown up listening to folktales by the fireside were still alive and well. Researchers collected and recorded their stories from the 1940s to the 1980s. Folktale collections were published one after another, including many books and picture books for children. However, some authors altered the old folktales. In the folk process, folktales change as they pass from teller to teller within the oral tradition. However, when an author has no background in the tradition, distortions can occur.

Television broadcasting of animated cartoon folktales started in 1975. The program *Japanese Folktales* was enormously popular because of its narrators, an actor and an actress. The show lasted twenty years. Through the animated cartoon, especially those unique narrative voices, the essence of the folktales reached people's minds and stimulated their nostalgia for old Japan.

In the latter half of the twentieth century, storytelling at home decreased. The tradition of large, extended families changed into a preference for small, nuclear ones. Hearthside culture was also changed by oil, gas, and electricity. Fireside storytelling, which had continued for a thousand years or more, virtually disappeared. However, there are still a few fireside storytellers who can tell in their district dialect without depending on books. They learned the stories from their grandparents by listening. As many as 120,000 tales are now preserved in Japanese folklore archives.

Storytelling in Communities and Homes

"Modern storytelling" began at the end of the nineteenth century in Japan. Modern storytellers learn their stories from books. The famous editor and author Sazanami Iwaya began to tell stories at elementary schools in 1898. Afterward many of his apprentices held story hours at grade schools, kindergartens, and public libraries.

Storytelling as a children's service at libraries began about 110 years ago. Since the Pacific War, libraries everywhere in Japan have offered storytelling courses. Librarians, teachers, and mothers are learning to tell stories. Mothers work as volunteer storytellers at libraries or schools. This activity also enhances interpersonal relationships in the local community.

The Japan Storytellers Association (*Katarite-tachi no Kai*) was established in 1977 to enhance storytelling in order to promote intellectual development of children and enrich their verbal environment. Storytelling is more powerful than reading aloud in encouraging and enriching children's imagination.

Storytelling in Japan Today

During the past twenty years volunteer storytellers in Japan have visited schools, kindergartens, homes for the aged, and so forth. The Japan Storytellers Association estimates that there are approximately 30,000 amateur storytellers throughout Japan. They tell folktales and stories for children and present *kamishibai* ("paper drama").

The majority of storytellers in Japan are librarians and volunteers. The few professional storytellers are invited to events and festivals where they perform on various stages, telling folktales. They also write, publish books on and for storytelling, and give lectures in various courses for storyteller training.

Traditional storytellers who tell in dialect still exist in various places in Japan. Some local governments offer folktale studies courses to train new storytellers to tell folktales in dialect and perform at municipal events or at sightseeing spots.

There are also some programs that broadcast folktales on the radio. These are very much loved by senior citizens. The listeners are surely happy to hear the old stories from various places. Folktales transmitted on radio reach their minds and carry the warmth of stories.

The Japan Storytelling Festival started in 1992. The Japan Storytelling Network supports this festival with the help of local governments. The 2006 festival had about 1,500 attendees. There were ten locations throughout the city at which any participant could tell during the festival. More than 450 stories were told. Happiness was shared through each other's words at the festival.

ABOUT THESE STORIES

The stories in this book come from a single source, yet they represent all of Japan. How can that be?

The source is Hiroko Fujita, who in childhood learned hundreds of stories by listening to the elders in Miharu, a small farming town in the mountains of Fukushima Prefecture. She is now respected by Japanese folklorists as a keeper and teller of traditional folktales in the *ohanashi obaa-san* (storytelling grandma) country style. While some of her tales are unique to Miharu, others have been collected by scholars throughout the length and breadth of Japan. It is that nationally representative group we offer here.

Some of these stories have motifs and plot elements that story-lovers will recognize. Many, however, have not appeared in English except in scholarly indexes, which unfortunately are now out of print. We hope that this book will provide a fresh and expanded view of life in the Japanese countryside of long ago, through the lens of story.

These stories are meant to be *told*. Please read them aloud, enjoy their different flavor in your mouth, play with them. Japan has an ancient tradition of high literature, but these country tales were told just for fun for children and village folk. Of course they have deeper meanings and teach important lessons, but none of that would happen if the stories weren't fun.

Hiroko Fujita comments about her story titles: "When I listened to stories as a child, I never cared about their titles. If I wanted to hear a story again, I just asked, saying: 'You know, the story where Tono-sama becomes a peach peddler' or 'That story of *Choro choro chorori*.' And the farmer next door knew what I meant. So every time people ask me 'What is the title of the story you have just told?' I have trouble. *Momo Uri* is commonly known as 'Wife's Portrait,' but I remember I enjoyed the peach selling scene better, so I decided to title it 'Peach Peddler.' "

About repetition, Mrs. Fujita says: "When you tell stories to adults, they quickly get tired of repetition. But children love it! For example, the part (in "Peach Peddler") where the farmer struck the field once, went back home, admired his wife saying 'What a beauty! What a beautiful woman!', went back to the field, struck once again, went back home, said

'What a beauty!', and went back to the field. When I listened to it as a child, that repetition was such fun. I also enjoyed the contrast between the man's lyrical chant and Tono-sama's blunt calling. No matter how many times my neighbor repeated the scene, I never got tired of it. As a child, what I enjoyed about this story was the many repetitions, rather than the story itself."

When we see them printed on the page, these repetitions can easily become tiresome. But when you listen to a story, you don't feel that way. That is one of the differences between "listening" and "reading."

Regarding the use of Japanese words, we wanted the stories to retain some of their exotic flavor, but we have kept the foreign words to a minimum in hopes that the text will be easy for English speakers to read aloud or retell. Japanese pronunciation rules are simple; see the pronunciation guide in appendix B.

Some Japanese words have become familiar: samurai, futon, tofu. The first time they appear, less familiar words are printed in italics with a definition in parentheses. Thereafter they are in regular print without the definition, but you can find them in the glossary in appendix B. Please try using them, and enjoy the special feeling they give to the tale.

The Japanese version of "Once upon a time," *Mukashi mukashi, aru tokoro ni* . . . . ("Long long ago, in a certain place . . .") , may be too much of a mouthful for American tellers, but you can easily say *Oshimai* ("The end").

Japanese traditional storytellers use many stylized sound effect words. A slithering snake always goes "*zuru zuru, nyoro nyoro.*" Softly falling snow is always "*non non,*" while something heavy falls "*poTON!*" These sounds, and any repeated chants, are printed in italics to distinguish them from text or dialogue.

Of course it is not necessary to use these traditional sounds when you tell the story in English, but if you learn some, they will add to the flavor of the tale. The glossary in appendix B includes a list of these sound effects, which you can use in the retelling of any Japanese story.

> For tips and ideas for using these stories in an educational setting, please consult appendix A.

You can learn a lot more about the stories from appendix A, "Comments and Notes." Mrs. Fujita provides "COMMENTS" on her thoughts, memories, and insights about the stories. Fran Stallings adds background research in "NOTES" and suggestions for telling the stories to English-speaking audiences. This appendix also lists the scholarly citations, which compare the versions collected across Japan.

Hiroko Fujita heard these stories sixty years ago from people who were then fifty or older, who had learned them in their own childhoods from elders who had been children in the mid-1800s when Japan first reopened to the outside world. The stories truly come from the Japanese countryside of another age. And they are just as much fun today.

MAP OF JAPAN

HOKKAIDO

HONSHU

Miharu

Edo/Tokyo
Kyoto
Kashiwa
Osaka
Nara

SHIKOKU

KYUSHU

PART 1

STORIES OF ANIMALS

Why are crows black? Why do owls sleep in the daytime? Why do swallows eat bugs? Why do dogs lift their hind legs when they urinate? Why do mice have buckteeth? People in the old days wondered about many natural phenomena and enjoyed inventing fanciful explanations.

Unlike the creation myths of ancient Japan, these stories are not religious in nature. Some versions mention "God" or "Buddha," but alternate versions of the same story credit another cause. People also told cautionary fables and endless tales with animal characters. But some country folk seriously believed that certain animals had magic power to transform their appearance and trick people; see part 6 for those stories.

OWL'S PAINT SHOP

A long, long time ago, no bird had any color. Sparrows, swallows, bush warblers were all white.

This was very inconvenient. Sparrow had a hard time finding his mate because he couldn't tell who else was a sparrow. It was also dangerous, because they couldn't hide in the green trees. On the green grass, they showed up like scraps of paper. It was such trouble that they all went to ask God for his permission to paint themselves in different colors.

God said, "I understand. It's a problem for all of you to be white. Very well. Go to Owl's paint shop and have him paint you in any color that you choose. But there has to be an end to everything, so I set seven days as the limit! For the next seven days, you may go to Owl and have him paint you."

The first bird who went to Owl was Bush Warbler. She said, "I like the color of fresh leaves just coming out in May. Paint me that color, please!"

Owl said, "The color of young leaves. As you wish. I'll paint you in that green." He took his paintbrush and painted Bush Warbler a fresh green color.

Next came Crane. "I like being white, but I want to try some red on my head. And also, it might look nice to have some black showing when I spread my wings. Paint me like that."

"Very well," Owl said. He used his red brush on Crane's head and black on the lower edges of Crane's wings.

Kingfisher came and said, "I would like many colors on me. Red here, yellow here, blue here, and green here. Paint me that way."

"As you wish," Owl said and painted him in many different colors.

Chinese Partridge said, "I like orange here and black here." She was painted that way.

Sparrow said, "I like to be modest," and he was painted brown.

Swallow flew straight down from the sky and said, "I like black and white. Divide them clearly."

Thus, Owl worked and worked, painting each bird in colors of its choice.

Owl's Paint Shop

Three days passed, and four days passed, but Crow had not come yet. He was so vain that he couldn't pick the color he wanted.

"Kingfisher has too many different colors. I don't like that. Should I try red on my head like Crane? Or should I try solid green like Bush Warbler?"

He wondered and wondered, and soon it was the evening of the seventh day. "Oh, my goodness! I have to hurry to Owl right away!" he said and flew to Owl.

First, he thought he would go for Bush Warbler green. "Could you paint me in the same color as Bush Warbler?" he asked. Owl painted him in fresh green.

But then Crow realized, "Well, in the woods you wouldn't be able to tell me from the trees. I don't like this color after all. I have changed my mind. Paint me in this bright red."

"Red," Owl said and painted him red.

Then Crow said, "It looks like I'm on fire. This will hurt my eyes. I want that modest brown instead."

"Brown," Owl said and painted him in brown.

But Crow said, "I look like a tree trunk. It's boring. I want that sky blue instead."

"Sky blue," Owl sighed and painted him in sky blue.

Crow kept on and on, "I don't like this. I want that." Yellow. Purple. Pink.

Owl kept painting over and over, but Crow was never satisfied with any color. Owl had to run busily among the big jars full of paint. Suddenly he tripped on a jar, and from that jar, black paint spilled onto Crow and covered him all over.

Just then, the sun went down. God declared, "That's the end."

So, Crow had to stay black ever after. And ever since, Crow has been angry at Owl. "Owl spilled the black paint and made me dull-looking. It's all his fault," he said. Whenever he saw Owl, he chased him.

Owl got scared, and would not dare to go outside in daytime. Even nowadays, Owl sleeps in the depth of the forest in the daytime and sneaks out only at night.

Oshimai! (The end!)

SPARROW AND SWALLOW

*O*nce upon a time, in the really old times, when Buddha appeared on Earth as a man named Sakyamuni, Sparrow and Swallow were sisters.

The older sister, Swallow, was very careful about her clothes and makeup. She always wore nice outfits, and she did only light work so that she wouldn't get her clothes dirty. But Sparrow didn't mind so much about her appearance, and enjoyed working hard in the fields.

One day they heard that Sakyamuni was sick in bed.

Sparrow thought he must be suffering, and she hurried to go visit him. She jumped out of the muddy rice field where she had been working. She hopped *pata pata pata* right over the head of her father, who was sitting beside the field. Covered with mud, just as she was, she hurried to Sakyamuni's house.

Meanwhile, Swallow took pains about her appearance before going out. She changed into a formal black kimono, put on fresh makeup, and fixed her hair. Then she set out from home.

Sakyamuni was very pleased that Sparrow had hopped *pata pata pata* to come visit him. He said, "It was very thoughtful of you to come so quickly, never minding your muddy clothes. In gratitude, I will give you permission to eat rice just like human beings."

So sparrows are allowed to eat some of the rice which humans grow for themselves.

But it was not good manners for Sparrow to leap over her father's head. Sakyamuni balanced the reward with a punishment for her bad manners. From that time on, sparrows cannot move their legs separately when they walk. They can only hop, both legs together.

When Swallow arrived at Sakyamuni's bedside all dressed up but late, he got very angry. "You may eat only earth and bugs!"

So that's what swallows eat now, and they sing,

"Tsu-chi kutt-cha, mu-shi kutt-cha. Shi-bui! Shi-bui!" ("Eating dirt, eating bugs. Nasty! Nasty!") [Try saying the Japanese words very fast; they sound like a swallow's call.]

Oshimai!

Sparrow and Swallow   5

THE TALE OF THE LIZARDS' TAILS

A long long time ago, when God was making the animals and human beings, he gave tails to dogs and cats and many different animals—but not to lizards.

The lizards thought it would be better for them to have tails when they walked, especially when they turned corners. So they went to God to ask if he had any extra tails.

God said, "As a matter of fact, I gave tails to human beings but they think their tails are of no use. I'll go to the humans and get the tails for you."

So God went to the humans and said, "Can I have those tails back?"

The humans said, "Yes, these tails are just a bother to us." And they gave the tails back to God. God adapted the tails from human style to lizard style, and put them onto the lizards.

The lizards were so thankful to God that they handed the story down from parents to children, from children to grandchildren. "This is the tail which the human beings gave to us. If ever they act like they want it back, we must return it."

So even a lizard of the present generation will drop his tail off and run away as soon as a human acts as if she wants it back.

But humans haven't been handing this story down from generation to generation. They don't tell their children that humans gave tails to the lizards, and so children nowadays don't understand why lizards drop off their tails when humans try to grab them. They think, "Lizards just leave their tails behind; that's their nature," when in fact this behavior is due to the way lizards have handed down the story and have taught their children, "We must return our tails to humans when we see them."

Oshimai!

THE FOURTH LEG

*O*nce upon a time, when God had just created men and animals, the dog had only three legs. Dog hopped about, thinking, "It's so hard to walk with just three legs! Everyone else has four, the cat, the mouse . . . . I would like to run around on four legs, too."

So he went to God to tell him his wish. "God, if you have one more leg left over, I would like to have it."

God searched in the box where he kept his things but he couldn't find any legs. He said to Dog, "Wait here, I'll go look for a leftover leg," and off he went.

First he came across a cat and asked him if he could give back one of his legs. "No indeed," said Cat. "If I didn't have four legs, I wouldn't be able to catch up with mice when I'm chasing them. I can't give you back one."

Next he asked Mouse, who said, "If I didn't have four legs, I couldn't run away from the cat. I can't give you one." God agreed with her and went on toward the mountains.

There he met Rabbit hopping around. "Rabbit, you are able to hop so fast. It wouldn't make much difference if you gave away one of your legs, would it?"

"The only thing I know how to do well is to hop away. I need all my legs for that."

He also met a deer running very fast. "Deer, would you mind giving me back one of your legs?"

"All I can do to protect myself is to run away fast. I can't give up any of my legs," Deer answered. God agreed and continued further into the woods.

He saw a boar coming slowly in his direction. "Boar, surely you can give me back one of your legs. You don't need them to run."

"Look at my huge body, God. I couldn't support all this weight with just three legs. I can't part with any of them."

God thought for a moment. "I know what I can do! I'll ask the human. The other day he gave me back his tail, so maybe he'll also give back a leg."

But the human wasn't pleased with what God asked him. "No!" he said angrily. "I have only two legs and if I were to give you back one of them, I would have to hop around on one leg. I can't do that."

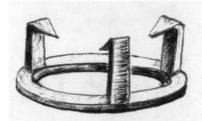

God was at his wit's end. He cried out loudly, "Hey, isn't there any one who is willing to give me back a leg?"

"I would," he heard from far away. He went in the direction of the voice.

It was an iron hearth trivet who said, "I neither walk nor run, so you can have one of my legs."

"Really? Then please give me your fourth leg. Thank you very much," said God.

And he adjusted that leg to the right length and put it on the dog, who was very much delighted.

"With four legs it's so much easier to walk! How thankful I am! I must take care of this leg that God found for me!!!"

And from that day on, the dog always raised his fourth leg when he peed.

Oshimai!

MOUSE TEETH

Millet is a small-seeded cereal grain used to make tasty dumplings, noodles, and other dishes.

Once upon a time, there was a weasel who decided to grow millet to store for winter. In the spring, he turned over the soil and planted the millet seeds. He took great care of them.

When autumn came, his field was full of ripe millet. The heads of grain were as thick as a tanuki's tail. Weasel was very happy at the sight.

"I will harvest the millet tomorrow," he thought, and went home.

The next day, when he came to his field to harvest his millet, it was already gone.

"Oh, who took my millet? I worked very hard and it grew so well. Who had the nerve to steal it?" He was furious.

He searched from one house to another. He walked and walked until he heard tiny voices coming from a burrow.

"It was so tasty, last night's millet cake.

"It was so tasty, last night's millet cake."

Weasel pricked up his ears. "Well, what's this?"

A small mouse came out of the burrow scampering *choro choro chorori*, singing. "It was so tasty, last night's millet cake."

The next little mouse came out *choro choro chorori*, singing, "It was so tasty, last night's millet cake."

Another came *choro choro chorori*. "It was so tasty, last night's millet cake."

Then, out came a big mouse. "Hush! Hush! Don't sing such a song outside," she said to her children.

Now Weasel understood. He started digging from the other side of the burrow. He dug and dug, and found a pile of millet hidden at the very end of the mouse burrow.

Weasel was furious. He caught Mother Mouse.

"Why did you steal my millet? I worked so hard to grow it!" He was almost ready to kill the mouse.

"Oh, oh, I'm very sorry. I just wanted to feed my children. I'm very sorry. You can take all the rest, please forgive me," Mother Mouse said.

Weasel got all the rest of his millet back, but he was still angry. "I'll kill this mouse!" He was going to bite her.

"Please, don't kill me. Oh, please! I must take care of my babies!" Mother Mouse begged.

He let her live, but he was still angry. "I will cut off your teeth so that you can't steal more millet!" He got his saw and prepared to cut off all her teeth.

She said, "Yes, I did wrong. You have a right to cut off my teeth. But if I lose all my teeth, I can't gnaw a hole through the wall of the storage building at the manor house. Just two teeth would be very much appreciated. Please leave two teeth for me."

Weasel started to feel pity. He decided to leave two front teeth on her upper jaw and two on her lower jaw. All the rest he cut off with his saw.

That's why mice have only two teeth in the front of each jaw.

But Weasel's mercy was his ruin. He stored his recovered millet at the very end of his house. Little by little, it seemed to disappear.

When he checked the room carefully, he found a tiny hole in the wall. The teeth he left for the mouse were so strong that even with only two pairs of front teeth, she could gnaw a hole through wood, packed earth, or anything.

Oshimai!

[For very young listeners, you can add actions and audience participation:]

> Weasel plowed the field. [Pretend to plow; encourage young listeners to mirror you.]
>
> Weasel sowed millet seeds. [Pretend to sow.]
>
> Weasel weeded. [Pretend to pull up weeds.]
>
> The millet grew well. [Raise right hand and then left hand.]
>
> The ripe millet heads swung heavily. [Wave both hands.]
>
> Weasel reaped the millet. [Pretend to reap the millet stalks.]
>
> Weasel bundled them up. [Pretend to bundle them up.]
>
> Weasel carried the bundles home. [Pretend to carry them on your shoulder.]
>
> Weasel put them away. [Pretend to close doors.]

"Now, I'm all prepared for the winter. I will take a nap." [Press hands together and put them on the side of your face.]

"Ahh, I'm awake now. I'm hungry." [Yawn and pat your stomach.]

"I will eat my millet." [Pretend to open the doors.]

"Oh, no! No millet! No millet! No millet! No millet!"

[Listeners, in the roles of other animals, can reply in this pattern:]

Weasel: Dog, Dog, did you steal my millet?

Dog: I never steal. *Wan wan* (Bow wow).

Weasel: That's right. You don't steal. Cat, Cat, did you steal my millet?

Cat: I never steal. *Niau, niau* (Meow meow).

Weasel: That's right. You don't steal. Pig, Pig, did you steal my millet?

Pig: I never steal. *Bu bu* (Oink, oink).

Weasel: That's right. You don't steal.

[—and so forth. Participating "animals" can add, "I eat bones/fish/scraps," etc. Then you can proceed with the mouse part of the story.]

EARTHWORM AND SNAKE

Way back when God had just created men and animals, snakes had no eyes. Instead, they had beautiful voices.

One day a snake was slithering through a field with his red, split tongue flickering *pero peroh, pero peroh* [flickering sound], and singing "A-AA-AAh, A-AA-AA-AAh, A-AA-AAh, A-AA-AA-AAh."

It was indeed a beautiful voice. His tongue went *pero peroh, pero peroh*, and the song went "A-AA-AAh, A-AA-AA-AAh, A-AA-AAh, A-AA-AA-AAh." But he had no eyes with which to see the beautiful world. "I wish I could see the sun and flowers. I wish I could! I really do!" Snake sighed and slithered, singing.

On the other hand, earthworms in those days had big eyes. But these were useless, because they lived in complete darkness underground. "It is no use having these big eyes down here," said Earthworm, digging his way through the ground. "Instead, I wish I had a beautiful voice. I could sing to keep myself company."

One day, this Earthworm happened to come across that Snake.

Snake said, "I don't need this voice. I want eyes."

Earthworm said, "I don't need these eyes. I want a voice."

So they said to each other, "Let's exchange them."

And they did.

Now that Snake had big round eyes, he could see the sun and flowers. He said, "I didn't know how lovely the world is. Oh, I'm so happy, so happy."

And he still slithers happily, but he can't get rid of his old habit of singing—although of course he has no voice. So his tongue just flickers *pero peroh, pero peroh*.

Earthworm is happy too, to have such a beautiful voice. Singing keeps him from feeling lonely as he digs. But we can rarely hear the song. He is too far down under the ground.

Well, you might be able to hear it, if you try on a warm spring day. Listen carefully. Sometimes, you can hear a little sound, *Kyu kyu kyu*. That's his song.

Oshimai!

SKY WATCHER

*O*ne winter, a fox went to look for food on a mountain. But he found no food.

He went to look for food in a river. But he found no food.

"I wish I could get something good to eat somehow," he thought hungrily. Then he got an idea. He visited his next-door neighbor, an otter.

"Mr. Otter, Mr. Otter, it's not fun for both of us to worry about food every day. Let's take turns. Today, you prepare food for both of us. Tomorrow, I'll prepare food for both of us. The next day, you'll prepare food. How about that?"

"Yes, yes. That's a good idea," Otter agreed.

Otter went to a river and caught two fish.

"Mr. Fox. Mr. Fox. Please come to eat dinner at my house tonight."

That night, they enjoyed the fish together.

The next day, Otter thought, "Today, I don't need to get food. I will just go to Mr. Fox's house. He will serve me dinner tonight."

He visited the fox. "Mr. Fox. Mr. Fox."

Fox was staring at the sky. "Guard the sky, guard the sky, never look down," he chanted. "Guard the sky, guard the sky, never look down."

"Hey, Mr. Fox. Mr. Fox."

"Guard the sky, guard the sky, never look down. Guard the sky, guard the sky, never look down."

"Hey, Mr. Fox. Mr. Fox!"

"Guard the sky, guard the sky, never look down. Guard the sky, guard the sky, never look down." Then Fox did not utter another word.

"Well, I guess Mr. Fox has a reason for this," Otter thought. He caught a fish for himself and ate it at home, alone.

The next day, Fox came to Otter. "Mr. Otter. Mr. Otter. Tonight is your turn to prepare supper. I'm terribly sorry about yesterday. Yesterday was the day for Guarding the Sky. On that day, it is a rule that I can never look down, or even answer. That was the reason. I'm terribly sorry."

So, Otter went to a river and caught two fish. He gave one to Fox, ate one himself, and said, "Mr. Fox. I'll come to your house for dinner tomorrow."

"Yes, please do so!" Fox replied and went home.

The next day, Otter went to Fox's house. Fox was staring down at the ground.

"Mr. Fox. Mr. Fox."

"Guard the earth, guard the earth, never look up. Guard the earth, guard the earth, never look up."

"Mr. Fox. Mr. Fox."

"Guard the earth, guard the earth, never look up. Guard the earth, guard the earth, never look up."

"Mr. Fox, Mr. Fox, you promised me that you would give me dinner tonight."

"Guard the earth, guard the earth, never look up. Guard the earth, guard the earth, never look up."

After that, Fox did not utter another word.

"Well, I guess Mr. Fox has a reason for this," Otter thought. He went home and ate supper alone.

The next day, Fox came to Otter's house. "Hi, Mr. Otter, I'm terribly sorry about last night. Yesterday was the day I had to guard the ground. On the day of Guarding the Earth, I can't look up or even answer. I'm sorry. But tonight is your turn to prepare supper. So let's eat together."

Otter had to go to a river and catch fish. He caught two fish and came back.

Fox said, "Oh, you are a good fisherman. You caught two already. How do you do it?"

Otter was rather angry at Fox, so he thought he would tease Fox a little. "Fish just come to you. All you need to do is to dip your tail in a river. They are attracted by it and will bite on it. You can catch as many fish as you want."

Fox pretended that he knew this already. "Oh, yes, right. You do that, too? That's the way I always do." He went back home.

Maybe Fox felt a little guilty and thought he would prepare dinner for Otter. Or maybe he wanted to eat more himself. We don't know the reason for sure, but anyway, that night Fox went to the river alone. He put down his tail into the cold water and waited for a while.

"Mr. Otter said that fish are attracted by a tail. But they don't seem to come right away."

He waited and waited. It was very cold water. His tail started to hurt. "Ouch! Maybe a fish bit my tail."

Then, another ouch! "Maybe that was the second fish."

Ouch! "There comes the third fish. It surely hurts my tail, but I should wait a little longer."

Ouch! "Here comes another fish!"

Hurting was still better than what happened next: His tail started to feel nothing. It was too cold.

"My tail has become very heavy. It must have caught many fish. Maybe I should go home. But maybe I should stay a little longer," Fox thought greedily. "I don't need to give Mr. Otter more than one fish. The rest will be all mine. I'll wait longer then."

Soon the river water started to freeze. His tail was frozen in. While he waited, the sky became lighter. Dawn was coming.

"That should be enough. Now it's time to go home."

But by that time the river was frozen solid. He couldn't move his tail.

He tried to pull his tail, but it hurt and hurt. He tried, and it hurt. He tried, and it hurt. "*Guenko! Guenko!* [sound of a fox crying]," he cried.

There came a man to the river. He was going to fish on the ice. "Why, there is a fox," he said and called people.

"This naughty fox! You are the one who always plays tricks on us." They started to beat him and slap him.

Fox tried desperately to escape. He pulled his tail with all his might. His tail broke off! Ouch!! But he escaped.

Sometimes you see a fox without a tail. Perhaps it is a descendant of this fox.

Oshimai!

BRACKEN AND SNAKE

*O*nce upon a time, a snake was slithering happily. Now that he had eyes, he could see all the beautiful things. He felt happy and went along, flicking his tongue in and out.

It was a warm spring day. He traveled so long that he got sleepy. So he fell asleep in the middle of a green field. It was such a pleasant day. He was sleeping peacefully.

Then, from right under where he was sleeping, a shoot of thatching reed started to grow. "Oh, it's spring and I feel warm. I will grow now," thought the reeds.

Reeds have a sharp-pointed shoot, and they grow very rapidly. Poking through the skin of Snake's belly, the reeds grew and grew. They grew and grew and grew and grew.

Snake woke up and tried to move. He felt pain in his belly. He tried to go forward, he tried to go backward. Either way, he realized his skin would be cut with the sharp blade of the reeds. "What can I do?" he wondered. He stayed there, very still. "I am trapped here, unable to move. I'm so sad," he cried.

But right under his head and tail, bracken ferns started to grow.

"Wait till we grow, Snake."

Bracken fern shoots are hairy and soft. With their fiddleheads curled, they grew and grew and grew and grew, up to Snake's head and tail. Then they raised Snake up high so that he could get off of the sharp shoot of the reeds.

Since then, snakes show their gratitude to brackens by behaving politely when they see brackens. So, when you go to the mountains and are afraid you might run into a snake, you should take a bundle of brackens with you and call out, "I have some bracken. I have some bracken."

Then, snakes will leave you alone.

Oshimai!

Bracken and Snake   **17**

MELTING GRASS

*O*nce upon a time, a man was traveling alone in the mountains. He saw a big snake in the distance. It was coming his way.

As fast as he could, he climbed up a nearby tree and watched, looking down. He saw another man coming his way. This man did not notice the snake.

While the first traveler watched helplessly from the tree, that huge snake swallowed the second man up!

Snakes can open their mouths very wide, but their bodies are slim. So when they swallow a human, you can see the shape of the human in their belly.

Watching from his tree, the traveler thought, "He ate that man up whole, and his belly is shaped like that man. Oh, that snake must feel stuffed!"

But the snake slithered, *zuru zuru, nyoro nyoro* [sound of slithering], and started to munch on some sort of grass growing nearby. To the traveler 's surprise, the human shape inside the snake seemed to melt away. The snake became as slim as before.

The traveler figured out, "That grass must help melt things in the stomach."

When the huge snake was gone, the traveler climbed down and picked some of the grass and went back to his village.

There, in front of a noodle factory, he saw a sign. "Big Eating Contest Today! The winner eats free and wins a prize!"

The man thought, "I have this grass which melts everything in my stomach. That means I can eat forever."

He went into the factory. There, several people were eating noodles frantically. Some had already eaten ten bowls, some even twenty.

The traveler said, "I want to enter the contest." They brought him a tray full of little bowls of noodles in broth.

He ate and ate, not even chewing. He slurped those noodles down whole! After the twentieth bowl, he felt like he would burst.

"Excuse me. I need to go to the next room for a while." He was going to eat some of the melting grass secretly, and then return to the contest.

But after a while, the contest people started to wonder, "What's wrong with that man? He said he would go to the next room for a while. We waited and waited, but he hasn't returned. What happened to him?"

They slid the door open.

They saw no man.

They saw a big pile of noodles wrapped in the man's clothes, as if it was wearing them.

You see, that grass was very specific. It only melts human bodies.

Oshimai!

THE MICE MAKE
A PILGRIMAGE

Part 7 shows how to illustrate this story with drawings or mouse puppets made from handkerchiefs.

Once upon a time in a village, four or five mice gathered and were talking together. "It seems that the humans go on a pilgrimage to the Great Shrines of Ise. Why don't we go too?"

"That's a good idea. I heard that it's often done in big groups. If we're going, we can ask our friends if they'd also like to come."

So each mouse went home and called, "Hey, you mice in the rafters, we're going on a pilgrimage to the Great Shrines of Ise! Would you like to come with us?"

Many mice came down from the rafters, saying, "Yes, we'll come with you!"

"Hey, you guys in the sink, we're going on a pilgrimage to the Great Shrines of Ise! Would you like to come with us?"

Mice poured out of the sink, saying, "Yes, we'll come with you!"

"Hey, you mice in the storeroom, we're going on a pilgrimage to the Great Shrines of Ise! Would you like to come with us?"

Many mice came out of the storeroom, saying, "Yes, we're coming too!"

"Hey, you guys in the sewer, we're going on a pilgrimage to the Great Shrines of Ise! Do you want to come too?"

And out of the sewer came many more mice, saying that they also wanted to come along.

So they all set out together. As they passed by a vegetable field a mouse called out to them, "Hey, where are you all going?"

"We're going on a pilgrimage to the Great Shrines of Ise. You want to join us?"

"Yes, we would love to!" So the vegetable field mice joined them, and off they went.

They passed by a rice field. A mouse asked, "Where are you guys going?"

"We're going on a pilgrimage to the Great Shrines of Ise. Do you want to come along?"

"Yeah, why not?" And the mice from the rice field also came.

As they were crossing a plain, a mouse called out, "Where are you headed?"

"We're going on a pilgrimage to the Great Shrines of Ise. Would you like to come along?"

"Yes!" So the mice from the plains also joined the group.

They continued their trip and came to a great river. "Oh no, how can we cross such a wide river? Look over there, some men are getting ready to cross in a boat. We could do the same thing. Just a minute, I'll go ask the ferryman."

And the boss mouse went over to the ferryman and asked if he could take them to the other side.

"I don't mind taking you," said the ferryman. "But you have to give me some money in exchange. Do you have any money?"

Well, they didn't. They had no choice but to swim across.

But if each mouse swam separately, they would be carried away by the current and drowned. The boss mouse thought that maybe if they all held onto each other it would be safer. He said to the others, "First I'll dive in and swim up to the surface. When I squeak, the next one can come in and hold onto my tail."

So the boss dove in the water, swam up, and squeaked twice.

Then the next one dove in and bit onto his tail, squeak squeak!

Then the next dove in and bit the tail. Squeak squeak!

Then the next dove in and bit the tail. Squeak squeak!

Then the next dove in and bit the tail. Squeak squeak!

Then the next dove in and bit the tail. Squeak squeak!

Then the next dove in and bit the tail. Squeak squeak!

Then the next dove in and bit the tail. Squeak squeak! There are still many more to come.

The next dove in and bit the tail. Squeak squeak!

Then the next dove in and bit the tail. Squeak squeak!

. . .

And if you go to that river, you can still see the mice at the end of the line, waiting to dive in.

Oshimai!

PART 2

STORIES OF VILLAGE PEOPLE

Listening to grandmother's stories around the family hearth

TABLE MANNERS

The farmers' names are based on numbers: ichi = 1, ni = 2, san = 3, shi = 4, etc. Many children know Japanese numbers from martial arts classes and will appreciate the names. The ending "-san" is like "Mr." in English; "-sama" is used for higher rank.

One year in a certain village, the farmers harvested plenty of rice. They were all very happy as they carried their crops to their magistrate.

The magistrate was happy, too. "Thank you. This year, I quickly collected enough rice for the land tax. It was easy and saved me a lot of trouble. As a small token of my gratitude, I want to invite you all for a small meal. I would like all of you to come to my house the day after tomorrow."

The farmers went home happily that day. But the next day, First Farmer Ichibei-san said to Second Farmer Nihei-san, "Nihei-san, Nihei-san, I can't go to the magistrate's party tomorrow."

"Why not?" asked Nihei-san.

"I didn't realize it until my wife told me. I don't know the proper manners for eating at such a big party! I would make a fool of myself. So, I can't go to the magistrate's house. Do you know any manners?"

"Of course not! I have never been to a formal dinner party."

They asked Third Farmer Sanbei-san.

"I don't know any formal manners, either," said Sanbei-san.

"Oh, what shall we do? We don't want to make fools of ourselves. But if no one goes to the party, we'll get in trouble with the magistrate. Ah, yes! Shoya-sama, our village head-man, knows everything. Let's go to Shoya-sama and ask him to teach us table manners."

So they all went to Shoya-sama and asked. He said, "Sure, I know what to do!" and he started telling them.

"The maids will serve each of you an individual tray with chopsticks, a bowl of soup, a bowl of rice, and side dishes of vegetables, fish, and pickles. But you can't just grab the chopsticks and start eating. First you must pick up your chopsticks properly." He showed them. "Lift them up with your right hand. Lay them in your left hand. Then grasp them with your right hand like this. This is how you pick up the chopsticks. You understand?"

"No, we don't understand."

"A little slow, are you? Very well, I'll show you again. Pick them up with this hand, support them with that hand, and re-hold them with this hand like this. You understand?"

"Umm . . . we think so." But they looked confused.

The lesson went on. "Pick up the soup bowl and take one sip. Put it down. Pick up the rice bowl and eat one mouthful. Put it down. Then, pick up the soup bowl, take another sip, and this time you can eat some of the chunks in it too. Put it down. Then, pick up the rice bowl and eat two mouthfuls. Finally you can start on the side dishes as you like! You understand?"

The farmers looked at each other in befuddlement. "No, we don't understand."

Shoya-sama explained many, many times. But they just couldn't remember it.

Shoya-sama gave up. "All right, here's what we'll do. I will be sitting at the head of the line, nearest to the head table. Ichibei-san, next to me, will watch and do what I do. Next Nihei-san will do what Ichibei-san did. Then Sanbei-san, and so on down the row. Just do exactly what the man next to you did, and you won't make a mistake. Let's do it that way."

Reluctantly, they agreed.

The next day, they got ready for the feast. They bathed, scrubbed, and soaked in the hot tubs. They dressed in their nicest, cleanest clothes, including brand new loincloths, which they tied around the waist, pulled between the legs, pulled through the waistband, and tucked in. Clean undershirt. Clean kimono. Clean socks. They looked good!

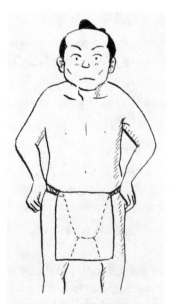

Traditional loincloth underwear

At the magistrate's house, they knelt at a long row of little tables. Shoya-sama sat at the first table on the right. Next to him sat Ichibei-san. Next to him sat Nihei-san. Sanbei-san, Shihei-san, Gohei-san, Rokubei-san, Shichibei-san, Hachibei-san, Kyubei-san, Jubei-san, and so on until Hyaku (one hundred)-bei-san sat at the end of the line.

Maids brought the trays of beautifully arranged food. It was time to eat.

Shoya-sama picked up the chopsticks with his right hand.

Ichibei-san watched Shoya-sama. "That's right. That's right. First thing was to pick up the chopsticks with your right hand."

Nihei-san watched Ichibei-san do that. "Now I remember." He picked up chopsticks with his right hand, too.

Sanbei-san did that. Shihei-san did it, and so on down the row.

Next, Shoya-sama laid the chopsticks in his left hand.

Ichibei-san thought, "That's right. Now you are supposed to set them in your left hand." Ichibei-san set them. Nihei-san set them. Sanbei-san set them.

Now Shoya-sama grasped them with his right hand.

"That's right. Now, you are supposed to hold them this way." Ichibei-san, Nihei-san, they all took them up with their right hand.

Shoya-sama lifted his soup bowl and sipped it once. Ichibei-san watched Shoya-sama. "That's right. First, you just sip soup." He picked up his soup bowl and sipped it once. Nihei-san watched and sipped his soup. Sanbei-san sipped his soup. So did the others.

Then, Shoya-sama picked up his rice bowl and ate a mouthful of rice. Ichibei-san thought, "Now I remember." He picked up his rice bowl and ate a mouthful of rice. Nihei-san, Sanbei-san, and the others ate a mouthful of rice, too.

Next, Shoya-sama picked up his soup bowl and sipped the soup again. This time he ate a piece of vegetable, too. "That's right. This time, you are supposed to eat something from the soup." Ichibei-san picked up his soup bowl. He sipped the soup and ate a vegetable. Nibei-san did likewise, on down the row.

Shoya-sama picked up his rice bowl and ate two bites of rice. Ichibei-san thought, "That's right, now it's rice again," and he ate two bites of rice. Things were going pretty well for all the farmers, Nihei-san, Sanbei-san, and so on.

Now Shoya-sama picked up one of the side dishes. It was his favorite, sweet potato in a sweet, slippery sauce. He picked up a bite-sized piece with his chopsticks. But before he could put it into his mouth, it slipped, fell to the floor—*poTON!*—and rolled away *koro koro koro*.

Ichibei watched.

"I see. That must be the proper manners. You are supposed to drop a piece of sweet potato like that." He dropped one—*poTON!*—and it went rolling *koro koro koro*.

Nihei san watched. "That's how you do it." *PoTON! koro koro koro*.

Sanbei-san imitated him, *PoTON! koro koro koro*. Shihei-san did too, *PoTON! koro koro koro*.

Shoya-sama thought, "No, no! That's not what you're supposed to do!" but he couldn't speak aloud. Instead he waved his hands frantically, trying to signal them to stop.

So Ichibei-san thought, "I see. You are supposed to wave your hands after dropping a piece of sweet potato." He waved his hands.

Watching it, Nihei-san, Sanbei-san, Shihei-san, and so on, they all waved their hands.

Shoya-sama was mortified. "This is terrible." He buried his head in his arms. "I'll run away to the storage house and hide," he thought.

But he stood up in such a hurry that he stepped on the tail of his loincloth underwear. It came untied and fell off as he ran to the storage house, covering his head in his arms.

Ichibei-san watched this. "I see. After you wave your hands, you're supposed to drag your underwear, cover your face, and run to the storage house."

He followed Shoya-sama. Nihei-san, Sanbei-san, and so on, they all dragged their underwear, hid their faces and ran to the storage house.

That was the end of the feast.

Oshimai!

PLANT OF FORGETFULNESS

Once upon a time, there was a very greedy innkeeper. He was not a religious man, but one day he did a very unusual thing: He went to listen to a priest's sermon. The sermon was about Chu-ri-pan-taka.

Chu-ri-pan-taka was one of the disciples of Buddha. His job was to sweep the paths in the Buddha's garden. He was a very simple soul who never learned to read or write. He forgot everything he was taught, even the things Buddha had taught him.

The older brother of Chu-ri-pan-taka was very smart. He never forgot anything he learned from Buddha. This brother said to Chu-ri-pan-taka, "You forget everything. You won't be able to go to heaven. You can't even write your own name. At least you should learn to read your own name!"

He took Chu-ri-pan-taka's clothes off and started to write his name on his body with brush and ink. "Your arms, Chu-ri-pan-taka, Chu-ri-pan-taka. Your shoulders, Chu-ri- pan-taka, Chu-ri-pan-taka. Your chest, your back, Chu-ri-pan-taka, Chu-ri-pan-taka, Chu-ri-pan-taka, Chu-ri-pan-taka." The smart brother wrote the name all over Chu-ri- pan-taka's body.

People laughed at him. They said, "Hey, Chu-ri-pan-taka! You look like you are carrying your name. Your name is all over you."

It didn't help. Chu-ri-pan-taka couldn't remember how to read his own name, let alone the precious scriptures Buddha taught them. "I have no hope of heaven," he sighed.

But Buddha said to him, "No, it's not hopeless. Smart people aren't the only ones who go to heaven. You work hard every day with this broom. Try to remember this broom, just this one thing. You see? A broom has a handle, a brush. You use it like this, sweeping. This is a broom. Even if it is in the closet, even if it's upside down, this is a broom. You see? Broom."

"I see. You sweep with it. It's a broom. You put it upside down. It's still a broom. I see. I see. Broom. Broom."

Chu-ri-pan-taka repeated the word broom. Broom, broom, broom, broom. He remembered just that one word, broom—and he died.

People buried Chu-ri-pan-taka with his broom. Then, after a while, a strange plant started to grow from the grave. First it just had big leaves, covered with strange marks like the writing on Chu-ri-pan-taka's body. Then, from the part close to the ground, a strange-looking bud came out. When it grew tall, its strange flower looked like Chu-ri-pan-taka's broom.

People said to each other, "What a surprise! This plant comes from Chu-ri-pan-taka! If we eat this plant, we might become as forgetful as Chu-ri-pan-taka."

"Oh, well. Even simple Chu-ri-pan-taka went to heaven. If we eat this, we may go to heaven too."

So people started to eat the crisp buds of this plant. They were very tasty, like ginger with a touch of garlic. They called it myoga, which means, "plant from a man carrying his name."

So, listen, people! You don't have to be perfect in everything. You only need to master one thing to go to heaven.

That was the priest's sermon. He meant that if you work hard and if you remember one thing, even if it is the only thing you remember, you can go up to heaven.

But that greedy innkeeper learned something different. "Aha! Eating myoga makes you forgetful! I learned something good."

It was the only thing he learned from the sermon that day.

The next day, a traveler arrived to stay at the inn. When this traveler sat down to untie his straw sandals, the wife of the innkeeper happened to see a big fat wallet in his jacket. She was even greedier than her husband. She told him, "Listen, listen! That traveler has a big fat wallet."

The innkeeper replied, "Oh, is that so? Yesterday, I learned something from the priest's sermon . . . . Now, let's serve myoga to this traveler. He might forget and leave his wallet here."

The wife was happy to hear that. She went to her vegetable garden behind the inn and picked many myoga. She started to cook them in her kitchen, *Koto koto koto koto. Kon, kon, kon, kon* [sounds of stirring and cooking].

She arranged everything on a tray. Miso soup with myoga. Myoga rice. Fried myoga. Myoga salad. Stewed myoga. Raw myoga. She brought the tray to the traveler's room.

The man saw the food and said, "Oh, my goodness! Is today's special myoga? I love myoga. Thank you! What tasty miso soup this is! And now, this myoga rice . . . . What a lovely flavor! How is this fried myoga? Oh, this is so good! Yum!! Oh, yes, myoga salad! Not bad at all!! This stewed myoga is good and raw myoga is very crisp. Yum, yum, delicious!! Oh, can I have another bowl of myoga rice?"

"Of course! Have as much as you like," the wife said, and brought him another serving.

The traveler ate everything.

"We've got it!" the wife thought.

That night, the traveler had a nice rest. When he got up next morning, he found another big tray for breakfast. Miso soup with myoga. Myoga rice. Sesami seed mixed with myoga. Myoga pickles. "Oh, yes? Another myoga special? I love myoga!" He finished everything on his tray. "I'm so full. Thank you. Thank you for everything!" he said.

Then he put on his sandals and left the inn.

As soon as he left, the greedy innkeeper and his wife rushed to the room where that traveler had stayed. "We gave him so much myoga. He must have forgotten something," they said, and looked around. But they didn't find anything.

"No, it can't be true. Aha, people tend to put their wallet under the futon sometimes. Look under the futon," they said and checked there. They even checked under the tatami mats, but they didn't find anything.

"It can't be true. He ate so much myoga. He must have forgotten about something and left it behind. Let's search more."

They looked and looked. Looked here, looked there, looked everywhere. But they found nothing.

Then suddenly, the innkeeper shouted, "Yes, he has forgotten something!"

"It worked?" his wife asked.

"Oh, yes. Oh, yes," he said.

"What? What did you find?" his wife asked again.

"Indeed he has forgotten. Myoga works so well."

"What is it?"

"He has forgotten to pay us," said the innkeeper.

Oshimai!

PEACH PEDDLER

*O*nce upon a time, there was a young farmer who was a very hard worker.

One day, when he was working very hard in his field as usual, a woman came walking by and the thong of her straw sandal broke. The man had a rag, which he had tucked into his belt to wipe his sweaty face and hands. It was as dirty as if it had been boiled for three years in muddy water! But he tore it up and fixed her sandal with it.

As he handed it back to the woman, he looked up and saw her face. What a beauty she was! He stared at her face and couldn't take his eyes away.

The woman stared at him, too. Finally, she said, "I want to be your wife."

How happy the man was! Right away he collected his sickle and hoe, and took her home.

After the wedding, they lived happily. But there was one problem. This young man, who used to work so hard, didn't go to work any more. From morning to night he just stared at his wife and said, "Oh, how beautiful you are! What a beauty you are!"

His wife told him, "Please go to the field. Weeds are growing."

So he went, carrying his hoe. He struck the ground once, then hurried back home. He stared at his wife and said, "Oh, how beautiful you are! What a beauty you are!" Then, he hurried back to his field.

Again, he struck the ground once, then ran back home. He stared at his wife and said, "Oh, how beautiful! What a beauty!"

He went back to his field. Again, he struck the ground once, then hurried back home, stared at his wife, hurried back to his field, struck the ground once, hurried back home . . . . Well, he never got his job done. Soon his field was covered with weeds.

His wife started to worry, and she got an idea. She hired an artist to paint her portrait from head to toe. She handed the portrait to her husband and said, "Hang this somewhere near the field. Then you can keep working."

He happily hung it on a tree branch.

He struck the ground and admired his wife's portrait. "Oh, what a beauty!"

He struck the ground again and said, "She is so lovely!"

Part 2: Stories of Village People

He struck the ground once more and said, "She is so beautiful!"

He worked, admiring her portrait every time he struck the ground. But he didn't have to go back home, so the job got done all right—until one day, a strong wind carried off the portrait. It flew over a mountain, across the forest, and he couldn't find it.

He gave up and went home.

Well, where did the portrait go? The wind dropped it into the castle garden of Tono-sama, the feudal lord of that region.

Tono-sama was looking at his garden from a balcony. He saw the paper fall.

"Something fell down over there. Go get it," he ordered his men.

One of his men brought it to the feudal lord. When Tono-sama laid his eyes on it, he couldn't take them off. "Oh, what a beautiful woman! What a beauty! This beautiful woman shouldn't be anywhere but in this castle. Find her and bring her here."

Dozens of men went to look for her. They searched and searched. Finally, they came to the farmer's house and tried to take her by force. But before they dragged her away, she pressed three peach stones into her husband's hand. "When they grow and bear fruits, come to sell them at Tono-sama's castle."

Saying so, she was taken.

In the castle, Tono-sama tried very hard to make her happy. "Smile. Smile at me."

But she never smiled after she was taken to the castle. She puffed out her cheeks, drew her lips tight, and made an ugly face.

Tono-sama asked her kindly, "Now, now, show me your lovely face as in the portrait."

But she didn't smile.

"Smile."

Still she didn't smile.

Tono-sama said, "Smile! I will give you delicious food. Smile! I will buy you a red kimono." He tried this and that, but she didn't smile.

Time went by.

Well, the farmer planted those peach stones and took very good care of them. After three years, the trees bore fruit. There is a traditional saying: Peaches, chestnuts, in three years; persimmons, in eight years; stupid pears, in thirteen. It means that peach and chestnut trees bear fruit in only three years, a relatively short time.

The man put ripe peaches in the baskets of his shoulder yoke. Carrying it, he went to the castle. But he couldn't get inside, because the guards wouldn't let him in. So he walked around the castle, calling, *"Momo, momo, momo iran ka na?* Peaches, peaches, don't you want some peaches?" in a singsong chant. "Peaches, peaches, don't you want some peaches?"

He called out loudly and walked around the castle. Around and around he went.

His wife in the castle heard him. Until then, she had looked sullen. But when she heard his voice, she smiled.

"Peaches, peaches, don't you want some peaches?"

Again she smiled. Every time she heard him calling, she smiled. She smiled and smiled, and she started to chuckle.

Tono-sama was very happy to see her laugh. He was delighted. "Yes, yes! She smiled! She smiled at the peach peddler's calling. Bring that peach peddler into the garden," he ordered.

The guard opened the gate and brought the young farmer in. In Tono-sama's garden, he walked around and around, calling, "Peaches, peaches, don't you want some peaches?"

The woman didn't just smile. She laughed *"Kekera kerakera,"* and laughed *"Hohohohoho, fufufufufu!"* and that made Tono-sama so happy.

"I see, I see, the peach peddler amuses you so much. If that is so, I will do it myself!" He snatched the shoulder yoke from the farmer and hollered in a flat voice, "Peaches, peaches don't you want some peaches."

But her face turned sullen again.

"Ummm, this wasn't good enough. Hey, give me your kimono."

Tono-sama put on the farmer's dirty kimono, and gave him his fine kimono.

Wearing the dirty kimono, Tono-sama carried the shoulder yoke and hollered, "PEACHES PEACHES DON'T YOU WANT SOME PEACHES!"

But she didn't smile at all. Tono-sama tried harder, "PEACHES PEACHES DON'T YOU WANT SOME PEACHES!" But she didn't smile. "Why don't you smile?" asked Tono-sama.

She answered, "It's not so easy to be a good peach peddler, is it? Maybe if you go around the village and practice, you might be able to become a fine peach peddler. Why don't you go out and practice?" She sent him out of the gate.

Then she told the guards at the gate, "That peach peddler might try to come back. But never let him in." She shut the gate tight.

After that, the woman and the farmer in Tono-sama's kimono lived happily ever after in the castle.

What happened to Tono-sama?

We never knew.

Oshimai!

MASK OF ONI

*O*nce upon a time, a mother and a daughter lived alone. They were very poor. The mother scratched out a living by sewing and doing laundry for the neighbors. Also she raised vegetables in her tiny garden. With all these, she managed to feed herself and her daughter somehow. But this hard work made her ill and she became unable to work. So her young daughter had to be sent out to work in a town on the other side of the mountain.

The mother packed her daughter's things in a woven wicker box. Then, from a pillar, she took down a mask of Otafuku, the happy woman. She put it in the box and told her daughter, "Think of this mask of Otafuku as your mother. Just like this mask, I will always be watching over you with a smiling face."

The daughter went to the town on the other side of the mountain, carrying the box with the mask in it. She became a babysitter for a very rich family. Early every morning, they tied the baby on her back. Carrying the baby all day, she swept the garden and washed diapers. She was a very hard worker, even when nobody was watching her. So the mistress in the house liked her very much.

When evening came and all the work was done, they untied the baby from her back. Then she went to open her box and talk to the smiling mask.

"Mother, were you watching me all day? Oh, you are smiling. You must be doing fine." Then she said "Good night" to her mother, closed the box, and went to sleep.

The other servants watched her talking into her box every night and thought it strange. "What is in there?" they wondered.

One day while the girl was working, they took out her box and opened it. There, they found the mask of Otafuku.

"Oh, this is what she is talking to every night. What a strange girl! Well, why don't we tease her a little bit?"

Somebody had a mask of the ogre, Red Oni. They put it in her box and hid the mask of Otafuku somewhere.

That evening, as always, the girl finished her work, put down the baby from her back, and went to open her box.

"Mother . . .". She was surprised. Her mother's face was Red Oni. "Something terrible must have happened to my mother!"

She hurried to the mistress and asked for a leave of absence to visit her mother.

The mistress said, "Of course you may go, but it is a long way over the mountain. You had better leave early tomorrow morning."

But she wouldn't wait. She just started running home, with the mask of Red Oni tucked in her jacket.

That night, a lot of gamblers gathered in the mountains. They made a fire and were gambling by the fire tossing their dice, *Jara-jara-bon*, *jara-jara-bon*.

Hoping that they wouldn't notice her, the girl tried to sneak past. But they found her and caught her by the neck.

"Hey! Why is a young girl like you walking alone in the mountains at this time of night? Where are you going? Are you a real human or an ogre in disguise? Are you really an Oni?"

She answered in a very faint voice, "My mother is sick. I was on my way home. Please let me go. Please."

But they said, "No, you can't go. You are a strange girl. Besides, our fire is going down. Stay here and take care of the fire," they commanded and put her right by the fire.

She had no choice. She fed the fire with the wood that the gamblers had collected. But the sticks weren't dry, so they didn't burn well. With her face close to the fire, she blew and blew. But only smoke and sparks came out.

As she blew, she remembered, "Oh, yes! I have a mask."

She put on the mask to protect her face and blew harder. After a while, the wood finally caught fire and the flames started to rise. The fire became bigger and bigger. The red flames shone on the mask, making it look very red.

As the flames flared, the mask looked as if it were moving. Red Oni looked as if it was alive.

When the gamblers looked at the girl after a game, they saw a scary Red Oni staring at them. The gamblers were so frightened. Throwing down all their coins, they fled as fast as they could.

The girl was blowing hard at the fire when she heard noises. When she took off the mask, all the gamblers were gone.

She saw coins everywhere. She picked up all the coins and waited for the gamblers until dawn. But they never came back. So she put the coins in her jacket front and her kimono sleeves and went home to her mother.

Her mother was perfectly fine. Her health had completely recovered.

And since the girl had brought a lot of money, she never returned to the town. Together, she and her mother lived happily ever after.

Oshimai!

DOCTOR WHO DROPPED HIS EYE

*O*nce upon a time, there was a village doctor. He was rumored to be a very bad doctor.

"Go to that doctor, and you will go straight to heaven," said villagers.

So nobody dared go to him. He had no patients and nothing to do. Day after day, he would just walk around the village.

One day, when he was walking around, a big dog came barking toward him. He hated dogs.

"*Wan wan wan*! (Bow wow wow!)"

He hurriedly climbed up a tree nearby. He climbed fast because he was so scared, but when the dog was gone and he looked down, he started trembling. He had climbed up too high. He couldn't get down.

"What shall I do? What shall I do?"

He was so scared that his hands and legs wouldn't stop trembling. Finally he fell down from the tree. He was unconscious for a while. Then he woke up and noticed that one of his eyes was gone.

"Oh, no! I fell down and dropped one of my eyes somewhere. If the villagers know I dropped my eye, my reputation as a doctor will fall even more. I have to find it."

With one eye, he searched and searched. Finally he found his lost eye in the grass. He looked around to make sure nobody was watching. Then, he threw the eye into his eye socket. But he was in such a hurry that he threw the eye in the wrong way. His eye was looking in at his body. He could see his insides very well.

"Oh, that's my stomach. And there is something next to the stomach, too. Oh, I can see blood circulating all the way."

He looked and looked.

"I see: Hiccups are the trembles of that part. If you eat too much, the stomach expands that much." He could see everything.

Now when villagers came and complained about their stomachache and headache, he knew very well about the inside of the body. With one eye, he looked into his own body, and with the other, he looked at his patient. Looking both ways, he could treat the patient well.

He got a high reputation and became very rich.

Oshimai!

BOY WITH A RUNNY NOSE

*O*nce upon a time, there was an old man who went into the mountains to cut green pine branches for New Year's decorations. He brought them into town to sell.

One day, he couldn't sell many. At the end of the day, heading home with an armful of leftover greenery, he crossed a bridge.

"There is no use taking these back home," he thought. "Maybe the god of water celebrates New Year's Day as we do." The old man threw his branches into the river below.

He started on his way home again when suddenly, he heard somebody call him from behind, "Hello. Hello." He looked back and saw a beautiful young woman.

She said, "Thank you very much for giving us those lovely green pine branches. My husband is so grateful that he wants to give you a reward. He sent me to bring you."

The old man just stood there, very surprised.

"Will you close your eyes for a minute? Hold my hand. Don't open your eyes until I say it's safe," she said and held his hand tightly. He closed his eyes.

He heard something rush by his ears. It sounded like a gust of wind or running water.

"Very well. You can open your eyes," the woman said.

He opened his eyes and saw a big, magnificent mansion in front of him.

"Please come in, please!" the woman said and led him into the house.

He followed her into a big reception room. The master of the house was there. He said, "Thank you for your gift of pine branches. This year, we can celebrate New Year's Day with proper green decorations. It's very hard to get them here. It's been a long while since we last had any. Thank you very much." He bowed deeply and said, "As a reward, please enjoy this feast."

They served the old man an elaborate formal dinner of three trays, each bearing dishes of beautiful, delicious food. He ate and drank his fill. "Thank you so much. I enjoyed it very much," he said and prepared to leave.

The master of the house said, "Perhaps it sounds like an unusual gift, but I know you don't have any children. I would like to give you one of my children."

"Oh, how strange! How does he know that I have no son to take over after me?" the old man puzzled. But he also thought it would be wonderful if he could have a child.

But when the master of the house brought forth a boy, the old man was shocked. The boy was so dirty. His arms and legs were filthy. His nose was running. His drool was running down his chin. He was smiling aimlessly with a loose mouth.

"Oh, is this the child?" the old man thought, disappointed.

But the master of the house insisted, "Please! Please take this boy. Make him your son. He is dirty, and his nose is always runny. But you must never bathe him nor wash his face. He is always picking his bellybutton. Each time he does that, he produces a *koban* (a large oval gold coin, worth quite a lot). But you must make sure he doesn't make more than one koban a day. And remember, keep him dirty. Don't wash his face and bellybutton."

So the old man took the hand of the dirty child with one of his hands, and the woman took his other hand. He closed his eyes. Before he knew it, he was in front of his house.

He opened the door and called his wife, " I'm back!" He explained what had happened. "So, I brought this child," he said.

As soon as the old woman saw the child, she exclaimed, "How dirty he is! He needs to take a bath right away."

"No, no. He must not. They said that we can't wash his face or his bellybutton."

"But look how dirty he is. Look at his kimono sleeves. They are shiny, because he wipes his runny nose with them," she said in disgust.

She couldn't help but wash the boy's arms and legs. Then, she took out an old kimono and made it into a new kimono for the boy. But that didn't help very much. The new kimono soon became dirty because the boy always had a runny nose and was constantly wiping it with his sleeves. Soon, she gave up trying.

But it was true that every day when he picked his bellybutton, a koban fell down from it. Soon they had a pile of koban.

They became richer and richer. They built a new house. They bought new kimonos. Their meals became more luxurious. Then, many people started to visit them. These new friends ate, drank, and danced happily together. It was fun.

But there was one problem: that dirty boy. They tried to keep him away from their guests, asking him to stay in a room at the back of the house, but the boy often wandered out of his room. He walked up to their guests, smiling aimlessly.

A guest might think, "Maybe I should say something nice to this child." Then the boy would wipe his nose with the guest's fine kimono.

This boy was so dirty that just seeing him made the guests lose their appetites. Little by little, the people started to stay away from the old couple. Soon, there was nobody who would visit them.

"Nobody comes to our house any more. It is all the boy's fault. If he were gone, they would come and we could have so much fun again."

"But if he is gone, we won't have money, and we won't live like this. If he could make more than one koban a day, it would be so much better."

The old man told the boy, "Try to make more than one koban a day. Try two or three kobans." But the boy just smiled at him as always. He only made one koban.

"All right. I'll try it." The old man picked the boy's bellybutton himself. But no more koban came out.

Instead, the boy collapsed and died.

"Oh, he is dead!!" they exclaimed. And they looked around themselves.

Their big house was gone. They were sitting in the middle of their old small, dirty hut.

Oshimai!

THE GOD OF POVERTY

*O*nce upon a time, there was a very honest man. He was a hard worker. Every morning, while morning stars were still in the sky, he went out to his vegetable garden. Every evening, even after the mountain crows had gone back to their nests, he didn't stop working. On rainy days, he worked in the house. On windy days, he worked around the house. He worked hard every day without taking a day off, not even a half-day. Still, his life didn't get easier at all. He remained poor.

Though he was poor, a matchmaker found him a wife from a village at the foot of the mountain. After that, he and his wife went up to their vegetable garden on the mountainside together. They cut weeds, turned over the soil, and carried up manure over and over, until their backs started to ache. They took such good care of their garden.

But when they planted seeds, crows dug them up. They had to plant seeds again. When the seeds sprouted, rabbits nibbled them. When the leaves grew, caterpillars swarmed on them. When sweet potatoes and daikon radishes grew big roots underground, wild hogs dug them up and scattered them around. When they brought their scant crops home, house mice ate them. Their life was miserable.

One December, this man and his wife were cleaning their house in preparation for the New Year.

"Our crops weren't much this year. But we were healthy. We shouldn't ask for more," they said as they cleaned their family altar.

Then they found something strange moving in the dark at the far back of the altar, *mosora, mosora* [scuttling sound]. What could it be? They pulled it out and dropped it on the floor.

It looked like a dirty, shriveled mouse. It made a face and rubbed its back.

"What are you?" the man asked.

The dried mouse replied, "Me? I'm the god of poverty."

"The god of poverty! How can you be a god? What on earth was a god doing back there?" they asked.

"I was preparing to move," replied the god.

"Move? Are you going to move to another house? Why are you moving?" They fired question after question.

"Well, it is a long story," the god said. And he began, "I didn't come here today nor yesterday. I came here when your father was still alive. Oh, I loved that time! Your father was lazy. He complained a lot, had backaches, and drank a lot. He didn't get up till the sun was high in the sky. Then he complained about aches here and there. In the evening, before the sun had set, he drank and gambled with his friends. If someone in the house complained, he started kicking and hitting. So no servant or field worker wanted to work here. One by one, they left. Soon everyone was gone. The house was covered with spider webs. The farm fields were covered with weeds. First the sunniest field, then the other fields were sold off to other families. When your father finally died, all you inherited was that vegetable garden in the mountains and a sunless rice paddy.

"I wasn't worried at all. The son of that man wouldn't carry the burden for three days, I expected. You would either leave this house and become a beggar, or hang yourself.

"But after three days, you hadn't hung yourself. After four days, you still didn't hang yourself. Maybe today, maybe tomorrow, I thought; I waited and waited. And then a bride came. She was such a nuisance. From early morning till late at night, she never took a break. In between the work in the vegetable garden and rice paddy, she cleaned the house, washed and mended the clothes. Your pots and pans started to shine. Every sliding door in the house got a fresh paper cover. The junk-filled storage room was neatly cleaned up and I couldn't find a napping place.

"So I went out to the garden in the mountain, and what a surprise! Once it had been covered with weeds. Now it was cultivated beautifully and seeds were planted. In a fluster, I called the mountain crows and made them dig out the seeds but I had little time to rest, because you planted seeds again, and they all sprouted. Right away I had to call rabbits and make them nibble the sprouts. When the leaves grew bigger, I had to call caterpillars. When sweet potatoes and daikon radishes grew bigger, I had to call wild hogs. In your house, I had to call mice. I was so busy that I didn't have time to rest at all. And I wasted away to skin and bones, as you can see.

"I'm so used to living here, but I can't risk my survival. So I decided to move and was preparing myself. That was when you caught me. Well, sorry I spoke so long. Farewell. Good-bye."

The god stood up and started to leave, heading weakly toward the door.

Suddenly, the farmer cried, "Wait a minute, please!" Then he asked his wife, "Well, what do you think?"

His wife said, "Yes, I feel sorry for him. We say there are myriad gods and goddesses in this world. Some do evil, like the god of illness and the god of anger. Even they are given offerings of rice with red beans once or twice a year. But I have never heard of worshipping the god of poverty. Wherever he goes, people will hate him. So why don't we ask him to stay here? We could think of it like taking care of an old sick father."

The man thought, "That's right. He has been living here from my father's day. He is not a total stranger to me."

So he said, "God of poverty, as you heard now, we want you to go back to that altar again. If you want to call rabbits and wild hogs, go ahead and do so. We just need to work harder." He picked up the little god with both hands and put him back in the altar.

From that day on, they started to put some of their meager food into a bowl and offer it to the altar, because it was they who had prevented the god from leaving.

"We have barley gruel today. Please have some."

"It's steamed millet today."

"We only have sweet potatoes today."

They kept making offerings and also they worked hard, starting so early that the morning stars still shone in the sky.

One year went by. Another year went by. Things started to change. When they planted seeds, they all sprouted. Nice leaves grew, and no caterpillars ate them. They made nice crops. When millet in other farmers' fields was still three inches tall, it was one foot tall in their field. The heads of millet looked like tanuki tails, swinging heavily in the wind, shining golden. It was a beautiful sight. Not only millet, but also sweet potatoes and daikon radishes grew very well. When harvest time came, the crops made huge piles.

The man said, "Oh, what shall we do? If we take all of this home, we won't have room to sleep."

He put the extra crops in bamboo baskets and gave them to their neighbors. "We got too big a harvest this year. I'm sorry to trouble you, but it'll be nice if your children help us by eating them."

But the next harvest, all the neighbors paid him back. "Thanks to what you gave us before, our children had plenty to eat and were able to help us farming. Our old father is feeling well again. So this year we, too, harvested many crops. We'd like to give you back some." Saying so, the neighbors brought him double or triple the amount he had given them.

"Now what shall we do? I guess we have to build a storage house," the couple thought.

The eldest man in their village came and suggested, "Your house is such a ruin. It's not a good idea to build just a storage house. You had better build a new house as well." So all the people in the village came to help. Some went to the mountains to cut trees. Some people carried the logs, others set them upright. Old people braided bamboo mats for the stucco walls or made ropes. Soon a beautiful, big house and a white-walled storage house were completed.

It was the morning of the day the man and his wife were moving to their new house. He looked up at their old house altar and said, "Our guardian god of poverty, by some turn of

Fortune's wheel, a new house was built and we are moving there today. We'd like you to move in there first. Please come down."

A very plump god of happiness jumped down from the altar.

"What? You are a god of happiness. I didn't call you. I have nothing to do with you. Our guardian is the god of poverty who looks like a dried mouse. God of poverty! Please come down here!"

The cheeks of the god of happiness flushed. He said shyly, "It's natural that you can't recognize me. I was like a dried mouse. I tried very hard to challenge you, but you wouldn't give in. The harder I tried, the harder you worked. Soon I found myself sending birds and animals away from your garden, telling them, 'This is not your place. Go back to the mountain.' Also, every morning and evening, you treated me to cooked vegetables, millet, rice, and so on. Thanks to them, I became as plump as this." He continued, "It's wonderful that you have a new house. I'd like you to keep taking care of me."

He ran out of the old house, stopped at the entrance of the new house, turned back, and smiled at them. Then, he entered the new house and disappeared.

Nobody has ever seen him since. But even today, the family in that house is living happily.

Oshimai!

TWO STRONG MEN

*O*nce upon a time, in a temple, there was a man named Niou. He was a courtyard sweeper and a very strong man. Nobody could match him at the sumo wrestling tournament in his village. He was so strong that he couldn't hold a thing without cracking or breaking it. Well, that's how strong a man he was. He learned that he was the strongest man in Japan.

So one day he asked his boss, the priest in his temple, "I have traveled many places to measure my strength, and I have learned that nobody could beat me in this country. I want to go to China and try myself. May I ask for leave?"

The priest said, "I see, I see. If you think so, go ahead and try. But remember, there are many different people in this world. Be careful not to be arrogant, and take care of yourself. I'm sorry I have nothing to give you. Oh, yes, I have a file here. I will give this file to you. Please take it with you."

Niou put the file in his jacket, and traveled by rowboat. He rowed and rowed the boat and finally got to China.

In China, he learned that there was a man named Dokkoi who was said to be very strong. Niou wanted to see him. He walked on and on looking for Dokkoi's house. When he came to a house, he asked, "Hello! Hello! Is this the house of Mr. Dokkoi?"

From inside there came out a little old woman. She was bent with age, and her hair was all white. She could barely walk. "Yes, yes, this is Dokkoi's house. Who are you?" she asked.

"I'm Niou from Japan. I heard Mr. Dokkoi is very strong. I came to have a strength contest with him. May I see him?"

The old woman said, "Oh, yes. But Dokkoi is in the mountains behind our home. He is cutting some trees. Please sit here and wait for a while." She pulled up a big stump and set it down in front of Niou. "Please sit here and wait," she said.

"Wow, even this old woman has such power," he thought. "Her son Dokkoi must be very, very strong."

And then, from a distance, he heard a voice. "Hooooy!!"

The old woman stood up and went around to their backyard. "Hooooy!!" she called back.

Then, Niou saw a tree flying toward them from the mountain far away.

At first he thought, "Is that a small branch?" But as it came closer and closer, he realized it was a huge long log.

The old woman caught it with one hand and put it down. Then another log came flying and she caught it and put it down. Then another, and then another. Finally, they made a mountain of logs.

Niou watched and thought, "Wow, if this old woman is so strong, I can't imagine how strong her son Dokkoi is. I would be a fool if I fought with him and lost my life. I think it's better to run away now." He started running toward the beach where he had left his boat.

Dokkoi came running after him. "Hey! I heard from my mother that you want to fight with me. Please wait! I want to see which of us is stronger. Please, please wait for me!" He came running after Niou.

Niou didn't want to wait. He ran and ran, and jumped into his boat. He started rowing his boat toward Japan.

At the beach, Dokkoi called out, "Please! Wait! Let's see which of us is stronger." He took a long chain out of his jacket, and threw it. It caught the bow of the boat. Dokkoi pulled it.

Niou rowed the boat. "He can't pull me back to the beach!" Niou rowed and rowed his boat.

But maybe Dokkoi was a little bit stronger than Niou. Little by little, the boat was moving back toward China and Dokkoi.

Just then, Niou remembered that he had a file in his pocket. He took it out and tried to cut the chain. *Giko, giko, giko, giko, giko, giko, giko, giko* [the sound of filing back and forth].

At the beach, Dokkoi was pulling the chain with all his might. Suddenly, the chain was cut off. *Po-ton*! Dokkoi fell back heavily on his backside.

And with that force, Niou's boat went zipping to Japan.

After he came back to Japan, he told people, "In China, there is a very strong man named Mr. Dokkoi." So Japanese people said, "I see, I see. If he is that strong, we will borrow his power when we pick up heavy things." So that's why whenever we pick up heavy things, we say, "Dokkoi, Dokkoi," the way other people say "Heave ho!"

In China, Dokkoi told people, "In Japan, there is a very strong man named Niou. He can break an iron chain."

So it is said that in China, whenever they pick up heavy things, they say, "Niou."

Oshimai!

Baka Musuko

The stories of Baka Musuko (Foolish Son) taught the consequences of thoughtless behavior. Children and adults alike were reminded by these tales to think ahead to the results of their actions, and to be sure they understood directions before acting. It was an enjoyable way to learn manners.

In telling these stories, you can call the foolish young man "Baka Musuko" as his name. It is comparable to "Lazy Jack" in English and Appalachian folktales.

FOOLISH GREETINGS

*O*nce upon a time, a foolish son was walking with his father. They came across an acquaintance. "Hello, what a beautiful day it is today," the father greeted the man, but the son just stood there looking the other way and picking his nose.

When they came home, the father said to him, "You are old enough to be able to greet people politely. It's not that difficult. You just have to say, 'What a beautiful day it is today.'"

"Oh, I see," said the son, and went out.

As he walked along, he saw a long line of people coming toward him. "Wow, look at all the people," he thought. "I'll show them that I know how to greet others!" So the foolish son said loudly, "What a beautiful day it is today."

But it turned out that it was a line of people going to a funeral. A man stepped out of the line and scolded him, "How dare you call it a beautiful day when our grandfather has just passed away!"

So he went home and told his father what had happened. "You are so foolish! In that case you should have said, 'I am very sorry, and I sympathize with you in your time of sadness'."

"Oh, I see," said the son.

The next day he went out again, and came across another long line of people. "This time I'm not going to make a fool of myself! I'll show them how polite I am," he said to himself, and said in a loud voice, "I am very sorry, and I sympathize with you in your time of sadness."

But alas, it was a bride and her relatives heading for a wedding ceremony. A man stepped out of the crowd and said angrily, "How dare you say that, when our only daughter is getting married today to a wealthy man in the next village!"

When he came home, he told his father what had happened. "You are such an idiot," the father said. "You should have said instead, 'How wonderful! Please accept my sincere congratulations'!"

"Oh, I see," said the son, and went out again the next day.

As he walked along, he saw a huge crowd of people. "There's a big crowd," he said to himself. "I'll greet them properly for once!" And so he cried out, "How wonderful! Please accept my sincere congratulations!"

But it was a house on fire that the people were watching, and out of the crowd came a man who said angrily, "How dare you congratulate me when my house is on fire! What's so wonderful about that?"

When he got home, he told the story to his father. The father said, "You are so foolish! When you come across a fire, you should fetch some water in a bucket and pour it on the fire."

"Oh, I see," said the son, and went out again the next day.

On his way there was a blacksmith's shop in which a blacksmith was blowing up a fire with bellows. At last the fire was strong enough for him to work, and he had just started to strike some iron in it when the son passed by.

"Oh no, there's a big fire! I'm sure they need some help!" He grabbed a bucket nearby, fetched some water from the river, and poured it on the fire.

"Hey, what do you think you're doing?!" the blacksmith shouted. "You put out the fire I made!!!"

When he got home, he told his father what had happened. "You are really foolish. When you see someone busy at work, you should get on the other side and strike with him. You should try to be of some help."

"Oh, I see," said the son, and the next day he went out again. On his way he passed by a house; inside he saw a couple fighting. The husband was hitting his wife on the head, and they were quarreling with each other. The son said to himself, "He seems to be busy striking. In this case I should get on the other side and help him." He ran in the house and started hitting the woman.

The husband, who had been striking her until then, got angry and shouted, "What in the world are you doing to my dear wife?"

He went home and told the story to his father. The father said, "I can't believe how foolish you are! If you see two people in a fight, you should get between them and convince them to stop. You should say, 'I'm sure you both have something to say for yourselves, but it would be better to make up for now'."

"Oh, I see," said the son, and went out again the next day.

He passed by a field and saw two bulls fighting with their horns locked together. "I should pull them apart," the son thought. He got between them and tried to pull them apart. He said, "I'm sure you both have something to say for yourselves, but it would be better to make up for now."

Well, the bulls didn't seem to understand him. They tossed him with their horns, and the poor son was badly hurt.

Oshimai!

Foolish Greetings

TEA-CHESTNUT-PERSIMMON-VINEGAR

*O*nce upon a time, there was a foolish young man. His father told him, "You need to learn how to earn money. Go to see your uncle in the mountains. He will teach you how to work."

So this foolish son went to see his uncle in the mountains. His uncle said to him, "Welcome, welcome. You have come at a good time. It is almost autumn. I have gathered many chestnuts. I made vinegar. I picked many persimmons and I roasted tea. Go to the city and sell them all. The autumn equinox holiday is coming, so people will make sushi. For that, they'll need vinegar. Guests will come, so the hosts will need to serve chestnuts and persimmons too. They will need tea because they will drink tea. I'm sure they will buy a lot of these things. Go to the city market and yell in a big voice, and I'm sure everything will be sold in a day."

The uncle put *cha* (tea), *kuri* (chestnuts), *kaki* (persimmons), and bottles of *su* (vinegar) into two baskets on a shoulder yoke. Before the boy started down the mountain to the city, his uncle cautioned him, "You can't sell if you don't remember what you are selling. Don't forget them." So on his way, this foolish boy kept saying, "Tea and chestnuts (*cha, kuri*) are in the front basket. Persimmons and vinegar (*kaki, su*) are in the back. Tea and chestnuts in the front. Persimmons and vinegar in the back. Tea, chestnuts, persimmons, vinegar. Tea, chestnuts, persimmons, vinegar. *Cha, kuri, kaki, su. Cha, kuri, kaki, su.*"

He went into the city market and put down his baskets. Then he called out in a very big voice, "Don'tyouwannabuy tea-chestnut-persimmon-vinegar? Don'tyouwannabuy tea-chestnut-persimmon-vinegar? *Cha-kuri-kaki-su, iran ka na? Cha-kuri-kaki-su, iran ka na?*"

People in the market wondered, "What is he saying? *Cha-kuri-kaki-su?* Tea-chestnut-persimmon-vinegar? What flavor is tea-chestnut-persimmon-vinegar? Do you know?"

"I don't know. I don't need such a thing."

So nobody bought any.

The foolish son moved to another market. There again, he called out in a loud voice, "*Cha-kuri-kaki-su iran ka na? Cha-kuri-kaki-su iran ka na?*" But again, nobody bought any. He moved from market to market several times. "*Cha-kuri-kaki-su!iran ka na?*

Cha-kuri-kaki-su!iran ka na? Don'tyouwannabuy tea-chestnut-persimmon-vinegar?" he kept saying. But nobody bought any.

The sun was going down in the west. He picked up the shoulder yoke and went back to the mountain. His uncle said, "What's the matter? Why didn't you sell anything? Did you call out in a big voice as I said?"

"Yes, I did, Uncle," he replied. "As you told me, I called in a loud voice, '*Cha-kuri-kaki-su iran ka na?* Don'tyouwannabuy tea-chestnut-persimmon-vinegar?' "

"Hey, hey, you can't say it all in one word like that. Nobody understands you. You have to say *'cha' wa betsu-betsu de 'cha'* ('tea' separate from 'tea'), chestnut separate from chestnut, persimmon separate from persimmon and vinegar separate from vinegar. Nobody would understand you if you say it all in one word."

"Oh, I see! I'll say that and sell them all tomorrow," the foolish boy said.

The next day, he loaded the shoulder yoke again as the day before. At the market, he put his baskets down and started to call in a big voice. But he was careful this time. "Nobody would understand me if I said it all in one word as I did yesterday. I won't make the same mistake," he thought.

So he called, *"CHA-wa-betsubetsu-de-CHA, KURI-wa-betsubetsu-de-KURI, KAKI-wa-betsubetsu-de-KAKI, SU-wa-betsubetsu-de-SU, iran ka na?"* [In English:] "Don'tyouwannabuy tea-separate-from-tea, chestnuts-separate-from-chestnuts, persimmons-separate-from-persimmons, vinegar-separate-from-vinegar?"

But nobody bought any.

Oshimai!

PICKLE BATH

In the old days, farm family meals ended with hot water poured in your rice bowl. After using a piece of pickle to scrub bits of rice into the water, you poured the liquid in succession into your pickle dish, vegetable dish, and miso soup bowl, then you drank this dilute soup—and put the rinsed dishes in a drawer under your place at table, ready for the next meal. Dishes were properly washed just once a week. Mrs. Fujita says that her family, from Tokyo, didn't follow this custom, but she saw it in the home of the old farmer Takeda Kuni. She notes that Buddhist temple apprentices still finish meals this way.

The pickle in this story is daikon radish pickled in rice bran and salt. Daikons grow a foot or more long and two to three inches in diameter. The pickles are normally served in round slices.

*O*nce upon a time, there was a young man. He was married, but had little brain. One hot summer day, he had an errand to visit his parents-in-law.

His mother taught him before he went, "Listen, my son. They will give you a feast. Then they will pour hot water in your bowl. Don't blow to cool the hot water: it's rude. Instead, pick up a daikon pickle with your chopsticks and stir the water with it. This will help the water to cool down. Also this adds a nice salty taste to the water. When the water becomes cool and tasty, drink it quietly. Do you understand?"

And off he went to his parents-in-law.

The day couldn't be hotter. When he arrived, he was soaked in sweat.

His mother-in-law said, "Welcome! I'm glad you came. You must be very hot after your long walk. Take a bath before dinner." She sent him to the bathhouse.

To see how hot the water was, he put his hand in the bathtub. It was so hot! So he yelled in a loud voice, "Bring me a daikon pickle! Please bring me a daikon pickle here!"

In the house, the old woman wondered, "What? Why does he need a daikon pickle when he takes a bath?" She was puzzled but anyway brought him a whole pickled daikon radish, the biggest one she could find.

The young man took the pickle from her and said, "Thank you very much." He went back into the bathhouse.

The old woman couldn't help being curious. "What is he going to do with that daikon pickle?" She went around back of the bathhouse, right behind the bathroom wall. Through a knothole, she peeked inside.

He was sitting by the tub, stirring the water with the huge pickle. *Kapporah, kapporah,* [sound of stirring] he stirred and stirred. After a while, he jumped into the water. He crunched the pickle with his teeth and drank the bath water. He crunched again and drank again. He crunched and drank, crunched and drank.

Finally he ate up the whole daikon pickle.

Oshimai!

SCARY SNACK

Mochi *(snack made of rice pounded into a completely smooth dough) is sometimes called* Mina-goroshi *(all killed), while* han-goroshi *(half killed) is another name for the sweet snack* botamochi, *whose rice center is only half-pounded. You can find recipes for botamochi and plain mochi in part 7.* Teuchi *(kill with a sword) is another name for* udon *(wheat noodles cut into long strips).*

*O*nce upon a time, there was a foolish son-in-law. He had some errands to do with his wife's family, so he went to see them. Everybody in his wife's family welcomed him warmly. His father-in-law, mother-in-law, grandfather-in-law, grand-mother-in-law all said, "Welcome. It's nice to see you."

They seated him by the hearth. He sat talking with his father-in-law. Then his mother-in-law came and whispered to her husband. "Do you like *Mina-goroshi,* or *Han-goroshi*? Or do you prefer *Teuchi*?"

His father-in-law replied, "*Han-goroshi* seems fine to me."

"Oh good, it's the fastest one," the mother-in-law agreed.

She went back to the kitchen, and with the grandmother, she started to work busily.

The foolish son-in-law had overheard her. He became very uneasy. Killing all, half killed, or killing with a sword? And they preferred half killed! He thought, "My life is in danger here. I have to leave."

"I happen to remember an errand. I must go," he said to his father-in-law, and stood up.

"Don't be silly. You just arrived. You must rest a while. Oh, yes, by the way, about your rice paddy. . . ," his father-in-law resumed his talk.

This son-in-law was so nervous. He stood up, sat down, stood up and sat down.

The mother and the grandmother saw him doing that and thought, "Oh, no! He is going to leave. We must hurry up!" In the kitchen, they worked even harder, making lots of clattering noise. Meanwhile the little grandson wandered into the kitchen and saw his mother and grandmother working busily. He looked at what they were making and thought, "It looks delicious."

But the grandmother told the boy, "This is a scary thing. Keep away from it." She sent the boy out of the kitchen.

The foolish son-in-law heard this. "Oh, no! They are making something very scary. Somehow I must get out of here quickly." He was so, so nervous.

But just then, from the kitchen the women brought something on a big plate. It was still steaming hot.

"If I eat this, I'll be half dead," he thought. He started to rise and said, "I'm not hungry. I'm full. I must go home now."

"Oh, really? We made you wait so long and now you don't have time to eat. Very well. If you must go," they said and put those botamochi, many of them, in a lacquered wooden box. They wrapped the box in a carrying cloth and handed it to the son-in-law. "Please take this with you. You can eat them at home," they said.

He had no choice. He had to carry them. He said good-by and left the house holding the package with his fingers at arm's length.

While he walked, he got afraid that the package might open a big mouth at any minute, and bite his hand. So he picked up a stick and tied the cloth wrapper onto the very end of the stick. He carried it on his shoulder and, looking back once in a while, he ran and ran. He ran so fast that the package slid down the stick and fell on his neck.

"Eeeek!! It's trying to bite me!!" he shrieked and threw the package away.

The botamochi spilled out of the box and broke open, revealing the white rice inside.

"Help! These scary things! They're coming to bite me with their white teeth!"

He didn't pick up the botamochi. He just ran through the woods all the way to his home.

Oshimai!

PART 3

STORIES OF PRIESTS AND APPRENTICES

Japanese Buddhist temples and monasteries used an apprentice system to train boys as priests or monks. A young apprentice worked for his master in exchange for lessons in literacy and scripture. Some boys had a genuine religious calling, but others (as in old Europe) were sent by families who couldn't support them. Defeated samurai sometimes saved their children's lives by apprenticing them in temples. Some masters were kind and generous teachers. Others, especially during hard times, begrudged every mouthful of food they had to share with their hungry, growing apprentices.

Temples in big towns, with wealthy patrons, could support highly trained priests who came from noble or samurai families. Poor country temples often struggled, however. They might have a barely literate priest who had learned his sutras (Buddhist chanted scriptures) by rote memorization.

"*Namu amida butsu*" ("Hail, Amida Buddha") is the most basic Buddhist chant, but "*Nanmaida*" represents the mumble that comes out when people either don't know their prayers or aren't paying much attention to their diction.

SUTRA OF THE MOUSE

Once upon a time there was an elderly couple living happily together in the mountains. But one day the old man died suddenly.

The old woman was very sad. She wanted to give him a fine funeral with recitation of a pious sutra so that his soul could go to paradise. But unfortunately there was no priest that far back in the mountains. She had to hold a simple funeral all by herself. "When a fine priest passes by some day," she thought, "I'll ask him to recite a holy sutra for my husband's soul."

Soon it happened that a young temple apprentice got lost in the woods. He knocked on the old woman's door. "Please let me spend the night in your home," he begged.

The old woman was delighted. "What good timing, young boy! I'm going to cook heaps of good things for you. You can eat it all and then afterwards I would be happy if you could recite a sutra for my husband." And she cooked a huge delicious meal for the boy.

"What shall I do?" the boy thought to himself with his mouth full. "I'm still an apprentice and I can't recite the Hoke Sutra nor the Kegon Sutra nor the Hannya Sutra. . . . Oh well, I'll get by."

After he finished eating, he went into the other room and prepared to chant. The old woman sat down behind him and waited.

The boy didn't know what to do. Well, he had to say something. "I can't help it. I guess I'll just chant *Nanmaida*," he thought.

He chanted in a monotone, "*Nanmaida nanmaida nanmaida nanmaida nanmaida nanmaida.*"

He glanced behind him and there sat the old woman with a grateful look on her face.

He droned on, "*Nanmaida nanmaida nanmaida nanmaida nanmaida nanmaida nanmaida nanmaida nanmaida nanmaida nanmaida nanmaida nanmaida nanmaida.*"

As he chanted, he saw a mouse creep into the room from a hole in the wall. He chanted, "*Nanmaida **he comes in** nanmaida nanmaida.*"

As he watched, the mouse crept all the way to the other side of the room and peeped into another hole in the wall. The apprentice chanted, "*Nanmaida **he peeks in** nanmaida nanmaida.*"

The mouse went, "Squeak, squeak."

The apprentice chanted, "*Nanmaida* **he says something** *nanmaida nanmaida.*"

Then the mouse went into the mouse hole and disappeared from the room. So the boy said, "*Nanmaida* **he goes out** *nanmaida nanmaida.*"

CHING! He struck his gong to indicate that the prayer was finished.

He turned around and faced the woman. She had tears running down her cheeks. "Thank you so much, thank you so much," she cried. "You know, I had always thought that reciting sutras was very difficult. But I think I can manage to recite this one. I could do it every evening for my husband. Thank you very much!!" She was very happy.

The next morning the boy went on his way, but from then on, the old woman chanted his sutra for her husband every evening.

"*Nanmaida* **he comes in** *nanmaida nanmaida.*

"*Nanmaida* **he peeks in** *nanmaida nanmaida.*

"*Nanmaida* **he says something** *nanmaida nanmaida.*

"*Nanmaida* **he goes out** *nanmaida nanmaida.*

"*Nanmaida nanmaida nanmaida.*"

CHING!

Thus, she chanted the sutra for her beloved husband.

One evening, two robbers passed by.

"An old woman lives all alone in that house. Here's our chance! We can sneak in and steal something," they said to each other. Very silently, they tiptoed to the house.

As they stepped into the entry, they heard a voice from the other side of the sliding paper door. "*Nanmaida nanmaida* **he comes in**."

The robbers stopped in their tracks at the door, very amazed.

They listened for a while, but the woman continued her sutra as if nothing unusual was going on. "*Nanmaida nanmaida nanmaida.*"

"Well, everything seems to be alright. I'll see what the woman is doing," one of them said. He poked a hole in the paper door and peeked into the room.

At that moment the woman said, "**He peeks in** *nanmaida nanmaida nanmaida.*"

The robber was astonished. "Hey, she was reciting the sutra with her back turned to me but she knew that I was peeping into the room!!"

"What are you saying? That can't be true! There is no way that she could know what you were doing!"

"It's the truth! That woman seems to see through everything. We'd better not go into this house. Let's leave her alone."

"No! We're not going to leave this place without stealing something."

There they were, whispering to each other, when they heard her say, "*Nanmaida nanmaida* **he says something**."

Hearing that, the two were scared out of their wits. "Let's get out of here! Who knows what she'll do to us!!!"

They turned around and started to go out when the woman's voice was heard, "**He goes out**."

The two robbers ran away as hard as they could, without looking back.

Oshimai!

THE FLOATING COFFIN

*O*nce upon a time, deep in the mountains, there was a temple so poor that the priest couldn't afford to have even one apprentice. His only companion was a striped orange cat named *Tora*, which means "Tiger."

But there came a time when there wasn't even enough food for the cat.

The priest said, "Tora, you have stayed with me for a long time, but now I've become too poor to feed you any more. If you stay with me, you'll starve. You are free to leave me and go anywhere you like."

To his astonishment, the cat replied, "*Nyah-nyah* (meow meow)! Thank you for taking care of me for a long time. To show my gratitude, I would like to do something for you. To-morrow, there will be a funeral for the daughter of a *choja* (rich man). They will have a problem and ask you for help. You should chant, '*Namu-kara-tanno, tora-nyah-nyah*'."

The priest did not pay much attention to Tora's words. After all, it was just a cat. And the ending of the cat's chant sounded like "tiger meow meow." What nonsense!

But next day, there was indeed a funeral for a choja's daughter. Many famous priests chanted sutras for her. Of course, the priest of the poor temple in the mountains was not invited.

When it was time to carry her coffin to the cemetery, the pallbearers raised the coffin onto their shoulders and walked solemnly. On the way, a strong wind came and lifted the coffin into the air! It stayed in the air and wouldn't come down.

The famous priests started chanting together, "*Namu amida butsu, namu amida butsu, namu amida butsu.*" They chanted and chanted with all their might, but the coffin did not come down.

The choja worried very much. "I can't let her stay in the air like that. These priests are not good enough. Send men for more important priests!"

They brought priests from the city. They brought priests from here and there. They brought all the priests they could think of.

The priests chanted all together, "*Namu amida butsu, namu amida butsu.*" But the coffin did not come down.

"Aren't there any more priests?" the choja asked.

"No, there are no more around here. Well, there is one more in the mountains. The very poor priest. But there is nothing he can do."

"That's all right. Just bring him here," the choja ordered.

Quickly, they sent for the priest and brought him to the cemetery.

His clothes were all torn. He was filthy.

"What can this priest do at all?" everyone wondered.

He looked around at the crowd, thinking, "Imagine, yesterday, my cat Tora was saying I should chant something. What was it that the cat said? Oh, I remember! It was *'Namu-kara-tanno, tora-nyah-nyah.'* Well, I'll try it."

He started, *"Namu-kara-tanno tora-nyah-nyah. Namu-kara-tanno, tora-nyah-nyah."* As he said this, the coffin in the air descended a little.

"Namu-kara-tanno tora-nyah-nyah." The coffin came down a little more.

"Namu-kara-tanno, tora-nyah-nyah,

"Namu-kara-tanno, tora-nyah-nyah,

"Namu-kara-tanno, tora-nyah-nyah,

"Namu-kara-tanno, tora-nyah-nyah,

"Namu-kara-tanno, tora-nyah-nyah."

Little by little, little by little, little by little, little by little, the coffin came down. Finally it landed on the ground.

At last they could bury the choja's daughter. He was very grateful. "Outside, you don't look impressive. But inside, you are the greatest priest of all. I'll join your temple. Let me be your parishioner," he begged.

So the choja joined the temple and it became very wealthy.

The priest and his cat Tora lived happily ever after.

Oshimai!

A DEBATE IN SIGN LANGUAGE

Konnyaku-ya is a person who makes and sells konnyaku, a tofu-like gel that is important in vegetarian diets. It is very bland but absorbs good flavors from broth.

This story must be told with the gestures shown in the diagrams on the following pages. For more detail about the Buddhist symbolism, see appendix A.

Once upon a time, there was a small temple deep in the mountains. That temple was so poor that the priest could not hire even one young apprentice. The priest lived and worked there all alone.

One day, a letter arrived from far away. It said, "Tomorrow, a high ranked monk from the capital will come to the temple to exchange Zen catechism with the priest."

The priest was so astonished! "Zen catechism? I don't know such a difficult thing! But if I can't answer his questions, I might be thrown out of this temple. Oh, no! It's terrible. What can I do? What?" In despair, he started to walk around the room. He paced this way and that way, round and round.

While he was doing that, the konnyaku-ya arrived to deliver fresh konnyaku. He called from outside, "Hello, priest!"

But there was no answer. So he went inside and found the priest walking circles in the main hall. "Hello, priest! Why are you pacing so frantically?" he asked.

The priest explained, "I received a letter from the capital saying that I have to meet a high ranked monk and debate Zen with him tomorrow. I don't know what to do. I'm in deep trouble." His face was pale.

"Oh, you are really worried," said Konnyaku-ya. "I am grateful to you for buying konnyaku every day from me. So, let me help you. Tomorrow, I will disguise myself as you, and do what you have to do."

The priest said, "Well, I am no better at this than you are. I will take a chance."

Early next morning, Konnyaku-ya came to the temple. He put on the priest's robe and stole. He sat in the main hall, pretending to be the priest. He knew he shouldn't say much because if he talked, the monk could tell he was not a real priest. So he sat in silence.

After a while, the monk arrived from the capital. He called from outside, "Hello. Hello!"

The real priest was in the next room shuddering with fear. The konnyaku-ya priest did not answer, either. He kept silent.

Hearing no reply, the monk decided to come in by himself. He came to the hall and saw what he thought was the priest. He bowed, "How do you do?"

A.

Konnyaku-ya priest bowed back silently. For a long time, they sat in silence. Then, the monk from the capital held his arms overhead in a big circle [see diagram A].

Konnyaku-ya replied by holding his hands parallel like this [see diagram B].

B.

C.

The monk held up both his hands extending all ten fingers, like this [see diagram C].

Konnyaku-ya held up just one hand with five fingers extended [see diagram D].

D.

E.

The monk then held up only three fingers [see diagram E].

Konnyaku-ya made a very rude face [see diagram F]!

F.

At that, the monk from the capital bowed deeply and said, "I admire you. Thank you very much." And he left.

The real priest, who was peeping through from the next room, did not understand what this was all about. He was surprised that the monk had already left. "Konnyaku-ya, Konnyaku-ya, what did you tell the monk?"

"I don't know for sure," replied Konnyaku-ya. " But he asked me if my konnyaku was round [diagram A]. And I replied that it was a rectangle [diagram B].

"Then he asked me if my konnyaku was ten *mon* [small coins used in the old days] [diagram C]. I replied it was five mon [diagram D].

"He asked me to sell it for three mon [diagram E]. I showed my rejection by making a rude face" [diagram F].

This didn't make sense to the priest. But anyway, the monk from the capital had left. Relieved and very happy, he thanked his friend Konnyaku-ya. That was it for the day.

Next day, the priest from the neighboring village rushed to the temple. He said, "To tell you the truth, I didn't think you were so good. But now I know that you are a very great scholar. The monk from the capital came by my temple yesterday after he met you. He said you were such a wise priest. He praised you so much."

"Oh, really?" asked the priest in surprise.

"The monk asked you, 'The Earth?' [diagram A]. You answered him, 'We don't live on all the Earth, just between the sky and the land' [diagram B]. It's so amazing, amazing. Then the monk asked you, 'How can we get to *Jodo*?' [the Ten Directions, Paradise] [diagram C]. And your answer was 'We must follow the Five Commandments' [diagram D].

"He asked you, 'What about the Three Thousand Worlds in which Buddha has taught?' [diagram E]. You said, 'If you have understanding, you can see all' [diagram F]. You are so wise. So wise."

The neighbor priest praised him and left.

Oshimai!

FU FU PATA PATA

You can learn about mochi rice snacks in Part 7.

Once upon a time, there was a Buddhist temple where two young apprentices lived with their master the priest. The apprentices' names were Chin-nen and An-nen. The priest worked them hard.

"Chin-nen, sweep the garden path!"

"Hai!" ("Yes sir, I heard you sir.")

"An-nen, polish the hallway floor!"

"Hai!"

"Chin-nen, read a sutra!"

"Hai!"

"An-nen, come and massage my back!"

"Hai!"

From early in the morning till late at night, the priest kept calling Chin-nen and An-nen. They worked hard, but the stingy priest fed them barely enough. They were always very hungry.

After he sent his apprentices to bed each night, the priest had a routine. He would stir the ashes of the hearth with the iron chopsticks that are used for arranging hot coals. He would dig out one of the mochi cakes he had hidden there in the afternoon, so that it would become warm and chewy on the inside, crisp on the outside. He would blow on the mochi to cool it, *Fu! Fu!* [blowing noise]. Then he dusted the ashes off of it, *Pata! Pata!* [brushing noise] and ate it with enjoyment.

In this way, he ate several mochi all by himself: *fu fu, pata pata, fu fu, pata pata.* He loved to do this every night.

Chin-nen and An-nen knew what he was doing because they could hear the noises. They peeped hungrily through a slit between the sliding doors.

"I wish I could eat that mochi."

"Oh, me too."

But they were not allowed to go into their master's room unless he called them by name. So every night, they just kept saying, "We envy the priest. We envy the priest."

One day, Chin-nen and An-nen got a great idea. They went to the priest. "Master, we want to change our names. Please give us your permission."

"Huh, how do you want to change them?" he asked.

"I want to be called Fufu."

"Ah, Fufu. And you?"

"I want to be called Patapata."

"I see. It doesn't matter to me what your names are. So you're Fufu, and you're Patapata. That's fine," said the priest.

That day, he worked them hard as usual.

"Fufu, wash the laundry!"

"Hai!"

"Patapata, sweep the veranda!"

"Hai!"

"Fufu, copy out a sutra!"

"Hai!"

"Patapata, heat water for my bath!"

"Hai!"

Night came. Both the apprentices went to bed. As usual, the priest stirred the ashes of the hearth with his iron chopsticks and found the mochi cakes he had put there in the afternoon.

"Here's one. Here it is. Fu! Fu!" He blew on it to cool it.

"Hai!" Chin-nen slid open the door and came in.

"What? I didn't call you."

"But you said 'Fufu.' I thought you needed me."

"Y-yes. I called you because I thought you might like mochi. Eat this." The priest had no choice but to give this mochi to the apprentice. So he picked up another one for himself. He dusted it, *pata pata, pata pata.*

"Hai!" An-nen came into the room.

"What? I didn't call you," said the priest.

"But you said 'Patapata.' You called me. So I came."

"I thought you might like mochi." He had to give the mochi to the second apprentice.

The priest appreciated their cleverness. After that, he never ate mochi alone.

Oshimai!

NEW HOUSE MOCHI

*E*arly one morning, a stingy priest hid many mochi in the ashes of the hearth. Then he said to himself, "Today a choja is having a ceremony to celebrate completion of the framework of his new house. It starts at noon and may last for hours. I'm supposed to go and pray for Buddha's protection of the new house. But I have just put many mochi in the ashes. I want to eat them . . . . Well, I have an idea! I'll send my apprentice in my place. He'll do all right."

The priest didn't know that the apprentice had seen him putting the mochi in the ashes.

He called the apprentice and ordered, "Go to the choja's and attend the New House Ceremony for me."

So the apprentice left. The priest waited for the mochi to be done. But before he could start eating, the apprentice came back.

"You are so early. Is the ceremony done already? And how did it go?"

The apprentice started to explain, drawing the house floor plan in the ashes with one of the iron chopsticks. "Oh, master, the choja is building an enormous house. You go straight inside and here is a big central pillar." He stabbed the iron chopstick into the ash. "Oh, master! What a surprise! I seem to have pierced a mochi with the chopstick."

"I put it there. I was going to give it to you when you returned. Now, eat it," said the priest.

So the apprentice brushed it off and ate it.

Then he continued, "The choja's house is in fact magnificent. When you turn the corner, there is a kitchen pillar right here." He stuck the chopstick in again. "Oh, I pierced another mochi!"

And he ate it.

"Then, you walk down the hallway. At the end of that, there is a stable. Here is a stable pillar." He stuck the chopstick in again. "I pierced another one!"

One by one, the apprentice ate all of the mochi.

Oshimai!

HOW MUCH RICE?

*O*nce upon a time, there was a very poor temple. The only time they could afford to serve rice was when they had guests.

Depending upon who the guest was, the priest decided how much rice the apprentice should cook. When the priest held up one finger, it meant the apprentice should cook one cup of rice. Sometimes he held up two fingers or five fingers. But most of the time, it was one finger.

Even so, the apprentice looked forward to having guests. Happily he would cook dinner. "Yes, yes! Today I can have some rice. It's not a lot, but still the priest will give me a portion."

One day the priest had a guest. They talked for a while, and then the priest went to the outhouse.

The apprentice waited eagerly. "How many fingers will my master hold up today? He hasn't shown me yet. Well, he might do it when he comes back from the outhouse." Thinking so, the apprentice followed the priest.

As soon as the priest entered the outhouse, there was a big scream. "Gyaaaa!!!"

The apprentice ran into the outhouse and saw the priest down in the toilet pit waving his arms high, struggling in there.

With a start, the apprentice ran back to the kitchen. He measured ten cups of rice, washed it, and started cooking it.

Since the apprentice ran off without helping him, the priest had to climb out of the toilet pit by himself. He stank so badly. He washed himself and changed his clothes. Then, he went to the apprentice and said,

"You! You didn't help me out. And you are cooking rice. I haven't told you anything yet. What are you doing?" the priest yelled.

The apprentice replied, "But master, you held up your ten fingers. I thought you were telling me to cook ten cups of rice. So I cooked it."

Oshimai!

Part 3: Stories of Priests and Apprentices

Elementary schoolchildren learning vigorous traditional folk dances

Hiroko Fujita telling folktales to elementary schoolchildren

**Thatched-roof house in which governor of Fukushima Prefecture lived
(see "Table Manners")**

Alcove in traditional room, displaying poem scroll, flowers, and artwork
(see "Fox Teakettle")

Old-fashioned hearth, set deep in the floor, with no chimney

Friends sharing a room in a traditional inn, sleeping on futons on the floor

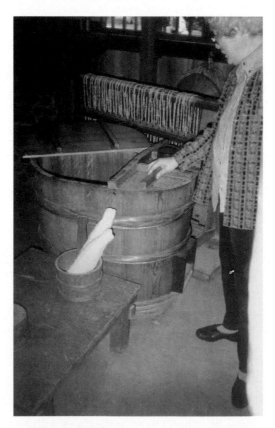

Old-fashioned wooden hot tub, with lid to keep water warm
(see "A Wife Who Doesn't Eat")

Intensively cultivated fields in which vegetables, fruits, and edible flowers are grown

Farmer using compact machine to harvest small rice field. Bundles of rice are hung by hand to dry.

Shichi-go-san (Seven-five-three) Festival: five-year-old boys and girls of three or seven years of age, at Shinto temples for blessing

Chrysanthemum Doll Festival: life-sized manikins wearing living, blooming plants

Modern family home

Friend helping tie *obi* sash of colorful summer kimono

Pounding steamed rice to make *mochi*—hard work

PART 4

STORIES OF STRANGE HAPPENINGS

A POET'S GHOST

Japanese poems can be very tricky to translate because poets often use puns whose multiple meanings all fit the context and add to the sense of the poem. This story depends on the double meanings of oki (glowing embers; ocean horizon).

Once upon a time, there was a poet. He was making a poem as he smoothed the ashes in the hearth. The first half of the poem went easily,

"Stirred all around
"Ashes do resemble sand
"Along the sea shore—"

He tried to think of a second half. "Mmmm, mmm . . . sand along the sea shore . . . mmm, mmm . . . ."

As he tried to think of a second half, suddenly he died.

His family held his funeral. But at midnight, the ghost of the poet appeared by the hearth chanting his unfinished poem:

"Stirred all around
"Ashes do resemble sand
"Along the sea shore . . . . Mmmm, mmm . . . resemble sand along the sea shore . . . mmmm, mmm . . . ."

Every night his ghost came. His family didn't know what to do. They talked to another poet.

That poet came to the house that night and waited by the hearth. The ghost appeared as always. The ghost started his poem again:

"Stirred all around
"Ashes do resemble sand
"Along the sea shore—"

"Mmmm, mmm . . . sand along the sea shore . . . mmmm, mmm . . . ."
Then the living poet made the second half:

"In the hearth we see the sea
"And embers as the ocean."

He had finished the poem.

"Thank you very much," the ghost said—and never returned.

Oshimai!

SPIRITS OF OLD THINGS

The goblin song sounds more mysterious if you use the Japanese words after explaining their English meaning. Start very quietly, getting louder and louder as the song repeats.

Once upon a time, there was a priest who was traveling alone. He came to a town.

"I don't have a place to stay tonight. Where shall I sleep? Oh, I see an abandoned temple over there. No one will mind if I stay there tonight." So he went in and went to sleep.

Midnight passed.

Around the Hour of the Ox [2:00 a.m., a traditional time for evil things to happen], he was awakened by strange voices from somewhere.

Furu kasa, furu mino, furu chiyochin
Furu kasa, furu mino, furu chiyochin
Furu geta, furu tabi, furu waraji.
(Old umbrella, old straw raincoat, worn out lantern,
Old umbrella, old straw raincoat, worn out lantern,
Worn out clogs, worn out socks, worn out slippers.)

"What is it? Where is it coming from?" the priest wondered.

He listened carefully. It seemed to be coming from under the floor. He pressed his ear to one of the knotholes in the wooden floor and listened carefully.

Furu kasa, furu mino, furu chiyochin
Furu kasa, furu mino, furu chiyochin
Furu geta, furu tabi, furu waraji.

The voices sang about many old things. The song grew louder and louder.

Furu kasa, furu mino, furu chiyochin
Furu kasa, furu mino, furu chiyochin
Furu geta, furu tabi, furu waraji.

Spirits of Old Things

It also sounded as if some dancing were going on under the floor. So the priest peeked through a big knothole. First he saw nothing but darkness.

After a while, his eye got used to it and he could see strange dancing shapes.

They were umbrella goblins, raincoat goblins, lantern goblins, clog goblins, and so on. Every goblin there was dancing to the song.

Furu kasa, furu mino, furu chiyochin
Furu kasa, furu mino, furu chiyochin
Furu geta, furu tabi, furu waraji.

Their dancing continued through the night. Then, when the morning came and the sky grew light, it suddenly stopped.

Under the bright morning sun, the priest checked under the floor.

Many, many things were stacked in there, such as old clogs with snapped toe thongs, old socks worn full of holes, old straw raincoats falling apart, old paper umbrellas with broken spokes, torn lanterns, and many other worn-out things.

The priest pulled out everything, set it on fire, and chanted a sutra, "*Namu amida butsu. Namu amida butsu.*"

All the worn out things turned to smoke and rose to heaven. And never again were those goblin voices heard haunting the abandoned temple.

So listen. Make full use of things, and when they get too old to use or repair, never just leave them. They will become goblins. When they become useless, you must burn them and make them rise to heaven. If you just keep them, they will haunt your house.

Oshimai!

YOU ARE WATCHED

*O*nce upon a time, a hunter carried his rifle into the mountains. On a tree branch, he saw a pheasant. He aimed his rifle and was about to shoot it. But he noticed something.

"That pheasant is staring at something. What is it staring at?"

He followed the gaze of its eyes.

There was a snake. Pheasants like to catch and eat snakes.

"I see. That pheasant is watching the snake. How stupid! It is so busy watching the snake, it doesn't notice that I am taking aim at it."

He watched the snake and noticed that it was staring at something.

"What is it staring at?"

He followed its eyes.

There was a frog. Snakes like to catch and eat frogs.

"I see. That snake is watching that frog. How stupid! It is so busy watching the frog, it doesn't know that the pheasant is watching it."

He watched the frog and noticed that the frog was staring at something.

"What is it staring at?"

He followed its eyes.

There was a worm. Frogs like to catch and eat worms.

"I see. That frog is watching that worm. How stupid! It is so busy watching the worm, it doesn't know that the snake is watching it."

Then he thought it over.

"That frog is watching the worm. It doesn't know that the snake is watching it. The snake that is watching the frog doesn't know that the pheasant is watching it. The pheasant that is watching the snake doesn't know that I am watching it. I who am watching the pheasant don't know . . . .

"I'm scared!"

The man screamed and ran back home.

Oshimai!

THE HOME OF THE
BUSH WARBLER

This version of the story is rich in detailed descriptions of the traditional celebrations for each month in Japan. For oral telling, you may want to compress or skip the details.

Once upon a time, there was a knickknack peddler. He carried a basket on his back full of combs, ornamental hairpins, needles, thread, hair cream, and such. He traveled from village to village selling these things to the villagers.

One warm spring day, this peddler was hiking over the mountain to the next village. On the mountain he felt a gentle breeze. He heard the lovely spring song of a bush warbler. He could smell beautiful flowers, too. "Oh, I should take a rest here."

He sat under a big tree. Enjoying the scent of flowers, birdsong, and warm sunshine, he dozed off.

A young woman came up to him. "Excuse me, Peddler. You shouldn't sleep here. You might catch a cold or something. My house is nearby. Please take your rest there."

She was such a beauty that he couldn't resist following her.

To his surprise, they came to a grand country estate behind the bushes. He hadn't noticed it before. The woman said to him, "Please wait on this verandah. I'll make some tea." She went in, and after a while, she brought him tea and delicious sweets.

He enjoyed them very much. Then the woman said to him, "You traveled over the mountains. You should take a bath." Again, he couldn't resist following her to the bathhouse. After he took a good hot soak, he didn't feel like moving an inch.

"Please stay here tonight," the woman said. Happily, he stayed.

The next morning he thanked the woman for her hospitality. He took out from his basket some combs, ornamental hairpins, and a couple of other things and gave them to her. He was about to say good-bye when the woman said, "I am all alone here. If you are not in a hurry, please stay another night."

He stayed another night.

The next morning, the woman said to him again, "Would you mind staying here another night?"

"Well, nobody is waiting for me at home."

Night after night he stayed there.

They were a young man and a young woman. Soon the woman became his wife.

Summer went by, autumn went by, winter went by. Every day she brought him a wonderful dinner, but he didn't know how she prepared it. Every morning, she brought a new kimono to his bedside, but he didn't know where she got the clothing, either.

"I can't live better. No worry about food nor clothes. This is like heaven, compared to the days I sold knickknacks in the rain," he thought, and stayed on.

Soon it was spring again. Flowers were everywhere.

One warm day, his wife told him, "I think I'm pregnant. I have to go back to my parents' home for a while. Please wait here. Behind the house, there are thirteen storehouses. So if you get bored, please enjoy looking at the old things we keep in there. Well, you may enter any of the houses from number one to twelve, any time. But to the house number thirteen, you must never go." She told him that, and departed.

For a couple of days, the man was comfortable doing nothing. But after four or five days, he got really bored and lonely. "There is nothing to do. I'm terribly bored! Well, my wife told me I could go and see those storehouses. Why don't I try that?"

He went to the first house and opened the heavy wooden door.

Inside the wooden door was a sliding paper-screen door. He slid it open. Inside was everything for celebrating New Year's Day. He saw a small altar on which was a big mochi offering. In front of that, on a hibachi, an iron kettle was bubbling. A *sake* (rice wine) server in the boiling water was full of sake at just the right temperature.

"Sake is ready," the peddler thought.

Next to the hibachi was a comfortable cushion and a little table laden with the special foods for the New Year's feast. He sat down and poured sake into its little cup. He ate sea bream, sea vegetables, cooked taros, and such. He stayed there all day. In the evening, he slid the inner door closed, shut the wooden storehouse door, and went back to his house.

"I played all day at New Year's Day. That was fun," he said and went to bed.

The next day, he managed to stay busy. But the next day, he became bored again. "Well, I will go and see what is in the second house."

He opened the door and slid the inner door open. Inside was everything for a Shinto shrine festival of February. Many red shrine archways stood in line. In front of that, on each side, were statues of foxes, the messengers of the god of grains. Many people were there to offer red rice or fried bean curd to the god. And for those people, there were many booths. Here was a booth selling masks, such as *Oni* (ogre) and *Otafuku* [happy woman—see "Mask of Oni"]. There was a booth selling good luck charms. Vendors called, "Good business! Good business! Don't you want it?"

Here was a booth for red lacquer ware. There was a booth for dumplings. A young woman at the dumpling booth was calling, "Come in! Have some tea!"

The man went in and had a cup of tea and a plate of dumplings. "Mmmm, that was delicious!"

When evening came, he shut the doors and went back to his room.

The next day, he managed to stay out of the storehouse. But the next day, he got bored again. "Well, I will go and see what is in the third house."

He opened the doors. Inside, he saw a beautiful display of dolls for the Doll Festival in March. On the top shelf were the emperor and empress. On the second row were three court ladies. Then came five musicians, the ministers of the Right and the Left, and three court servants. Below that were statuettes of an old couple representing a long healthy life, and a girl doll dancing with wisteria flowers.

In front of this gorgeous display he found sweet white sake, cakes, and special mochi.

"Oh, they look delicious. Allow me some."

The man drank and ate. "Oh, it was fun."

He slid the inner door closed, shut the wooden door, and went back.

The next day, he managed to stay out of the storehouse. But the next day, he got bored again. "I will go and see what is in the fourth house."

Inside, the cherry trees were in full bloom. People had spread straw mats under the trees and were enjoying picnics. The mountains in the distance looked hazy with pink and white blossoms.

"Hello, there! Please come and drink with us!" a man in one group called him. So he went there and had sake and sweet rolled omelet. Then, a man in another group called him, "Now you have to join us," so he went there and danced with them. He went from one group to another. Here and there he had sake.

When the evening came, he slid the door closed, shut the outer door, and went back.

He spent the next day at home, but the day after that, he became anxious to go to the storehouses again. "I will go and see what is in the fifth house."

Inside, there were carp streamers to celebrate Boys' Day in May. Irises and sweet-flag were in bloom. Boys wearing toy samurai helmets were playing with swords of long sweet-flag leaves. Somebody had prepared a portable hot tub and an old man was taking a bath scented with sweet-flag leaves, enjoying sake as he soaked. The peddler had sake with him. When he had had enough, he closed the doors and went back.

The next day he stayed home. But the day after that, he said, "I will go and see what is in the sixth house."

So he went, opened the doors, and went in. Inside was the season of rice planting. Young women had their sleeves tied back with red sashes. They wore red petticoats and sedge hats. They were standing in a tight line in a rice paddy, planting out rice seedlings.

"I will help you a little bit." The man went from this rice paddy to the next, planting rice hip-to-hip with the young women. After they finished, they served a feast of red rice and bamboo shoot rice, and called him, "Please join us."

So he went there and had red rice, sweet sake, bamboo shoot rice, and cooked butterbur leaves until he became full.

"Oh, that was a lot of fun."

He closed the doors and went home.

The next day he stayed home, but the day after that he said, "I will go and see the seventh house."

He opened the doors, went in, and found *Tanabata* [Star Festival, July 7—see cover illustration]. There was a big bamboo tree decorated with many long papers on which people had written their wishes. Earlier, young women had washed their hair with sweet-flag leaves. In the evening, they tied back their scented hair and came out with round fans in their hands to catch fireflies. Young men followed them with bamboo sweepers in their hands, catching fireflies too. In the rice paddy, frogs were croaking.

An old man in the distance called him, "We are having thin *somen* noodles for summer. Please join us. You have to eat somen on Tanabata."

So he went there and had somen and sake. Enjoying the Milky Way in the sky, he closed the doors and went back.

The next day he stayed home, but the day after that, he said, "I will go and see the eighth house."

He opened the doors. It was the Bon Festival when the souls of the dead come home to check on their living relatives. On a tray, cucumber horses, eggplant cows, and other vegetable dolls of animals were prepared. Over there, people were enjoying merry Bon dancing. On a scaffold, a young man stripped to the waist was drumming a big drum. Beside him were people blowing flutes. Around the scaffold, young women in their beautiful summer kimonos were dancing. Young men in sedge hats were also dancing. These men and women sent signs to each other as they passed by. Those who had made an arrangement disappeared two-by-two. As the night grew late, the dancing circle became smaller and smaller. Only old men and women were dancing in the end. Then, it was time to eat.

The peddler gorged himself on botamochi, sake, and a lot more.

Completely full, he closed the doors and went back. "The moon was beautiful, which reminds me that next month, we will celebrate the 256th night, the full moon of the ninth lunar month."

He stayed home the next day, but the day after that he went to the ninth house. Inside, it was night. The bright moon was shining. Silvery pampas grass heads swayed in the breeze as if they were inviting the moon. On the verandah he found a heap of dumplings on a tray. There were plenty of chestnuts and persimmons; it looked as if they were prepared for him. So he sat there alone, eating the snacks and watching the moon. Then he went back.

He stayed home the next day, but, the day after that, he wanted to go to the storehouse again. He went to the tenth house.

When he opened the outer door, he heard loud festival drums, *Ton ten, teke-teke*. When he slid the inner door open, he saw people carrying a portable shrine on their shoulders. "Oh, they are having a festival!" They carried the shrine here and there along the street. There were many booths.

The man enjoyed scooping goldfish at one booth, ate cotton candy at another, and had a supper of konnyaku and vegetables simmered in savory broth. He enjoyed the music and drumming.

He closed the doors and went home again.

After a few days he went to the eleventh house. There stretched golden rice fields. Rice ears hung heavily. In the fields, farmers cut rice with sickles. Then they hung the crops to dry.

"They look really busy today. I can help them a little bit."

He cut rice, carried the bundles, and climbed the drying scaffold. Finally, they finished everything.

"Please have harvest mochi."

So he shared mochi and sake, and had a good time. He slid the inner door closed, shut the outer door, and went home.

He stayed home the next day. But the day after that, he couldn't resist going to the storehouses again. He went to the twelfth house, opened the doors, and found people busily preparing for the New Year. Some people were pounding mochi. Other people sat adjusting the length of new kimonos for their children to wear on New Year's Day. Some were sweeping soot from rafters over the hearth. Others were making New Year's wreaths with straw and bamboo leaves. Some were fixing thongs on their new clogs.

"I'm back!" called a man returning from the mountains, bringing home a young pine branch.

"Have some of this warm soft mochi," they invited him. He had many kinds of mochi garnished with toasted soybean flour, sweet bean jam, or sesame seeds.

"This sake is an offering to God," said an old grandpa, "but we have to check it first." So they had sake, too.

He felt very happy. He closed the doors and went back.

He stayed home the next day. But the day after that he became bored.

"Well, I saw the twelfth storehouse. I suppose I'll have to start again from the first."

He thought, "The first one was New Year's Day. The fourth, they loved drinking! In the fifth that sweet-flag bath was good. In the sixth they were busy planting rice, but the sweet sake was delicious. In the seventh the young women were beautiful with their hair still wet. We caught fireflies. Bon dancing in the eighth was also fun. The moon in the ninth was beautiful. The festival in the tenth was colorful and fun. So were the people in the twelfth, preparing for the New Year."

He kept remembering this and that. "Which one shall I go to again? I have seen them all—except storehouse thirteen. My wife said I couldn't see that one. But that only makes it more interesting.

"Well, I won't go in there. I will just peek. It should be all right."

He went to the thirteenth storehouse and opened the outer door quietly. He heard nothing. It seemed pretty dark inside.

Just a little, he slid open the inner door. He couldn't see inside very well, but there seemed to be a plum tree blooming, as in very early spring. And from that tree, a bird flew out past him.

"Did something fly away?"

He stepped in. When his eyes got used to the darkness, he saw a bush behind the plum tree. In that bush, he found the nest of a bush warbler. And in that nest there were eggs.

He touched them. They were still warm. That bird had been sitting on them.

"It was a mother bush warbler that flew away. Where did she go?"

Suddenly, he felt a warm breeze.

The storehouses, the bush warbler, the house, and everything else were gone.

He was just sitting under that big tree by the mountain path, basking in the warm sun and smelling the scent of flowers.

The house and the beautiful lady had vanished.

When he came down to the village, people told him that three years had passed since he had set out into the mountains with his peddler's pack.

He tried to look for the house of the beautiful lady, but he never could find it.

People say that the strange estate appears only once a year, on a very comfortable spring day.

They call it "the Home of the Bush Warbler."

Oshimai!

SNOW WOMAN

*O*nce upon a time, a man hiked over three mountains to a town. After he finished his business there, he was going to return to his village. It was already afternoon.

The town people suggested, "It's winter and the day is short. You should stay here tonight and start tomorrow early in the morning. If you start now, the night will surely fall before you reach your village."

"I can walk fast and I know the way very well. I'll be all right even if it gets dark," the man said, and started on his way home.

It was not dark yet. But by the time he had crossed the first mountain, the clouds had covered the sky and it started to snow.

"Oh, there are thick clouds all over. It looks like it will keep snowing. I must hurry." He walked faster.

It kept snowing softly, *non non, non non, non non, non non.*

It seemed to snow forever, *non non, non non, non non, non non.* The man walked faster and faster, as fast as he could. He knew he had to hurry.

He walked and walked. Soon he noticed that the place seemed unfamiliar. But he had to keep going.

He walked and walked, until he saw his own footprints. "Oh, I walked here just a little while ago. I must be going in a circle. I'm in trouble. The path is buried deep in snow. The more I walk, the more I'll get lost. I know what: I'll dig a pit in the snow and stay there until the morning."

So he dug a pit, and was about to get into it. Suddenly, he thought he heard a baby crying somewhere: "*Hon-gyaa, hon-gyaa!!*" It sounded nearby.

But the snow was falling so heavily, *non non, non non, non non, non non,* that he couldn't see well.

"Strange. It can't be a baby crying. What is that sound?"

He walked in the direction from which the sound was coming. Within a few steps, he found a beautiful young woman holding a baby, standing in the snow.

"What on the earth are you doing here?" asked the man in surprise.

"I got lost along with my baby. I don't know what to do," said the woman.

"Oh, I'm sorry. I got lost, too. I made a pit there. So why don't we wait there till it gets brighter again. That's better than walking in the dark. Come, come this way," he said.

The woman said, "I left my baggage under the pine tree over there. I couldn't carry it all because my baby is heavy. Can I go to get it first?"

"Oh, sure. I'll wait here," he said.

"I'll be back soon. Could you hold my baby while I go?" she asked.

"Sure. What a lovely baby!" he said and took the baby.

The woman walked off in the direction of the pine tree. But it snowed so heavily, *non non, non non, non non, non non,* that soon he lost sight of her.

He waited there holding the baby, thinking she should be back in a minute.

When you hold a baby, you think it is very light. But when it falls asleep, it becomes much heavier. This baby fell asleep, and it became heavier and heavier for the man. He wanted to change his arms but somehow the baby stuck to his arm and he couldn't change his position.

"Oh, this baby is heavy. She should be back soon. The pine tree is right over there. She couldn't get lost," he thought and waited.

The baby was small and cute, and it kept sleeping. But it became heavier and heavier.

The man couldn't stand up any more. He sat down in the snow with the baby in his arms.

It kept snowing, *non non, non non, non non, non non,* and his arms became colder and colder. He could move his arms no more. He became sleepy with the baby in his arms.

"I shouldn't fall asleep. If I do, I will freeze to death. I must not sleep here," he fought. But the baby was so heavy. He couldn't move.

The woman did not return.

He was so sleepy.

He stayed there with the baby in his arms.

One day passed. Two days passed. But he never returned to his village.

People were worried about him and started to search for him in the mountains.

They found him frozen in the snow, with a thick piece of ice in his arms.

So, if you are asked to hold a baby in the snow, never, ever dare to hold that baby.

Oshimai!

PART 5

STORIES OF YAMANBAS

*Y*amanba (also called *Yama-uba*) literally means "old woman of the mountain," but some translators use "witch," "ogress," or "sorceress." Picture books show her dressed in rags, with wild white hair and a fanged mouth gaping from ear to ear. She can also transform herself into a harmless-looking younger woman or granny.

There are many indications that Yamanba was once a powerful nature goddess who controlled harvests, wild game, and weather. She taught humans the arts of spinning and weaving. She still helps women in distress and teaches people—sometimes the hard way—to respect nature.

In some stories, *Basama* (old woman, granny) has magical powers that imply that she is really Yamanba. Some of those stories are included here.

MR. SUN'S CHAIN

*A*long time ago, there was a house where a mother lived with three children. One day, the mother said she was going to go on an errand. She told her three children, "While I am not at home, put a pole in the door and do not open it. Yamanba may come here. Yamanba has a hoarse voice, and her hands are rough, so you can recognize her easily. Only open the door for me." And she left the house.

The children put a pole in the door sill, so that the sliding door could only be opened when they lifted the pole.

After a while the three children heard the door rattling, *gatagata, gatagata*! They thought it might be their mother.

But the oldest child paused before opening the door and said, "No! We don't know whether it is our mother or not. So I will ask." And he said, "Are you our mother?"

They heard a hoarse voice outside, "I am your mother."

So the oldest child said, "Oh! With such a hoarse voice, you must be Yamanba."

Yamanba thought, "They can recognize me by my hoarse voice. So I will change my voice."

She went back to the mountains. She mixed the eggs of mountain birds with honey and drank the mixture.

She came to the children again and rattled the door, *gatagata, gatagata*!

The children said, "Mother!"

The middle child was going to open the door. But the oldest child said, "Wait, wait. I will ask whether it is our mother or not." And he said, "Are you our mother?"

"I am your mother." The answering voice was sweet.

So the middle child said, "It must be our mother. Let's open the door, let's open the door."

When the middle child touched the pole, the oldest child said, "No! Wait. It may be Yamanba. So while I raise the pole in the door a little bit, you look out of the door carefully."

And the oldest child raised the pole a little bit. The door opened a little space, enough for a finger to enter. Yamanba tried to open the door by putting her finger into the space.

The middle child looked at her finger and shouted, "Oh! The hand is very rough!" And the oldest child fastened the pole of the door firmly.

So Yamanba's finger was pinched in the door, and Yamanba shouted, "Ouch! Ouch!" and she went back to the mountains.

Yamanba realized that her rough hands had given her away. So she pounded mountain yam and rubbed it onto her hands many times, and she came back to the children.

She rattled the door again, *gatagata, gatagata*!

The children said, "Mother!"

So the oldest child said, "I will ask whether it is our mother or not. Are you our mother?"

"I am your mother," Yamanba answered sweetly.

And the oldest child unfastened the pole a little bit, and the door opened a little space that a finger can enter. Yamanba put her finger in. Her finger was very smooth.

So the children said, "It is Mother!" They took off the pole and opened the door.

And a pretty mother entered.

The children thought, "Mother must have brought presents for us."

But she said, "I am very tired." She picked up the youngest child and went to the back room.

The oldest and middle children thought, "Phooey! She didn't buy any presents for us."

Then they heard a strange noise, *garigari garigari* [crunching noise].

They said, "Hah! Mother is clever. She is eating something all alone." They shouted, "Give us something to eat!"

The mother threw something to them. It was a bone.

So they peeped into the room and they saw Yamanba gnawing on the youngest child, *garigari garigari.*

They ran away out the back door in a hurry.

And Yamanba ran after them, still gnawing the bones of the youngest child.

The oldest child climbed the tree in the backyard as fast as he could. The middle child began to climb the tree, too, but he could not climb well. So the oldest child shouted, "Put your feet and your hands on the tree trunk and come up." This helped a little, but the middle child could not climb fast.

So the oldest child unfastened the rope which he wore instead of a belt, and tied the end of the rope to a branch, and hung it down. The middle child used the rope to come up to that branch, then the oldest child hung the rope from a higher branch and they climbed higher.

At that time Yamanba came to the bottom of the tree and demanded, "How did you climb?"

The oldest child teased, "We stood on our heads and climbed upside down."

"Like this?" Yamanba said and began to climb with her head down. But she could not climb well this way.

She demanded again in a threatening voice, "How did you climb?"

Because the middle child was scared of her voice, he said, "I put my feet and my hands on the tree trunk and came up." So she put her feet and her hands on the tree and came up.

She climbed for a while. But because her body was very heavy, she slipped down the tree. She demanded again with a threatening voice, "How did you climb?"

Because the middle child was scared of her voice, he said, "If you use the rope, you can climb." Yamanba caught the end of the rope and came up.

She came up one step . . . and two steps . . . .

As she came closer to the children, they fled to the upper branches.

At last they came to the top of the tree, and they thought, "Oh! We don't know how we can escape any further from here."

They saw the sun shining gently down, *chika chika.*

The oldest child shouted with a loud voice, without thinking, "Mr. Sun, Mr. Sun, could you hang down *kusari nawa* [literally "iron rope"—a chain]?"

Mr. Sun's Chain

All of a sudden a chain slithered down from the sun, *suru suru suru.*

So the children held onto it and swung up to the sky.

Yamanba saw that, and imitated the children. She said, "Mr. Sun, could you hang down *kusare nawa?* Mr. Sun, could you hang down *kusare nawa?*"

And a rope fell down from the sun. Yamanba held onto it and went up.

But because she had said *kusarE nawa* [a rotten straw rope] instead of *kusarI nawa*, it broke halfway and Yamanba dropped—*STON.*

And her red blood splattered the ground.

After that, buckwheat grew out of the place.

That is why the stalk of buckwheat is red now.

Oshimai!

A WIFE WHO DOESN'T EAT

*O*nce upon a time, there was a man who was well past the age of marriage, but he remained single because he was a very stingy fellow who thought a wife would eat up his food.

People tried to find a match for him. "How about that young lady there?" "How about this girl here?"

But he replied, "Oh, no. I don't want a wife. A wife eats rice. She spends my money, too. I don't want to have a wife." But still, people tried to make a match for him. So he said, "I will get married if there is a woman who doesn't eat."

One night, somebody knocked on the man's door. He opened the door and saw a beautiful young woman standing there. Her long hair was tied behind her back. She had such a tiny mouth. In a lovely voice, she said that she had lost her way and asked for lodging for the night.

"I will let you stay the night if you don't eat," said the man.

"No, I won't eat anything," said the woman. So he gave her a night's lodging.

Next morning when he woke up, he found that breakfast was already prepared for him. The woman was smiling beside his breakfast table.

"You don't eat, do you?" asked the man.

"No, I don't eat," said the woman, and she smiled with her tiny mouth.

When the man came back from his work in the forest he found his dinner ready, and the woman was smiling beside him. The man asked her if she would eat with him.

"I don't eat," said the woman.

The man, thinking her a really good woman, asked if she would marry him.

"Yes," she replied, "I want to be your wife."

Well, could it be true that she didn't eat? The man wondered, but he decided to marry her.

Next morning when he woke up, he heard sounds from the kitchen. The room was all cleaned up. His breakfast was ready. His bride sat beside his table, smiling, and watched him eat. He ate many helpings of rice. But still, she just smiled and watched him eat.

When the man came back home from his work that evening, his dinner was ready. Again, she sat beside him and smiled. She didn't eat a bite.

Every day it was like that. The man started to feel guilty. Once, he asked his wife, "Don't you want to eat with me?" But she just shook her head, smiling with her tiny mouth.

The man was very happy. He bragged about her to his friends. "My wife is the best wife in all of Japan. She is beautiful. She works very hard. She doesn't eat at all. She is the best."

"But don't you think it's strange?" his friends said. "All humans take food in at the mouth, and it comes out from the bottom. That's natural. If she doesn't eat anything, she might be some unnatural evil creature. You had better watch out."

The next morning the husband, becoming uneasy over his friends' remarks, pretended to go out for work in the mountain but came home secretly to watch his wife's behavior. He went around behind the house, climbed up into the rafters, and peeked down inside.

His wife cleaned the house and did her chores. Then she went to the storage house. She carried out a big bag of rice and poured the rice into a big pot, *zaza zaza* [sound of pouring rice]. She took it to the well. She washed the rice.

Kassya, kassya, kassya [sounds of washing rice]

Kyukyu, Zazazaza.

Shakka, shakka, shakka, zazazaza.

Shakka, shakka, shakka, zazazaza.

She put the pot on the stove and started the fire.

Bo, bo, bo, bo [sound of flames].

The husband in the rafters wondered, "What is this? What is going on? Have we invited people over for dinner today? She is cooking so much rice."

He kept watching. After the rice was done, she opened the lid of the pot. She took some rice in her hand and started to make rice balls as big as baby's heads. She put them on the pot lid. How many rice balls, we don't know, but she made many, many, firm rice balls and put them on the lid of the pot. After she had finished, she took the ribbon off her hair and let her hair hang loose. She divided her hair from the center. On the top of her head there was a big mouth. She threw a rice ball into the mouth, *Pon!*

She munched, *Amu, amu, amu.* She swallowed, *Gokun!*

She threw in another. She chewed and swallowed, *Musha, musha, musha. Gokun!*

She threw more rice balls in, *Pon, pon, pon, pon.*

Musha, musha, musha, musha. Gokun!

Pon, Pon, pon, pon,

Musha, musha, musha, musha. Gokun!

In a few seconds, she had thrown all the rice balls into the mouth on top of her head. After she had finished, she tied her hair at the back of her neck again. She looked as if nothing had happened.

The husband in the rafters started to tremble for fear at this sight. He almost fell, but somehow stayed there and tried to calm himself. It took a while. Then he climbed down at the back of his house and went to his storehouse where he had kept bountiful sacks of rice. He found that those sacks of rice were almost gone.

He did not know what to do, but went back to the mountain and thought it over.

In the evening, he came home, pretending that he had worked in the mountain for the whole day. He sat in front of the wife and said, "I want to divorce you. Please leave me."

"Oh, yes?" the wife said. She did not seem surprised. "If you want to divorce me, I would like to take one thing from your household when I leave. Is that all right?" she asked.

He was glad that she would leave peacefully, asking for just one thing. "That's fine. That's fine. Go ahead. Take anything you like."

"I want the hot tub," his wife said.

Just the hot tub? It was no problem. "Go ahead. Take it."

A Wife Who Doesn't Eat

No sooner had he said so, than his wife turned into the wild woman Yamanba. She ran to the bathhouse, picked up the empty wooden tub, caught the man by his neck, put him in the tub, put on the thick insulated lid, and ran toward her home in the mountains carrying the tub on her shoulder.

The man in the tub struggled to get out. But the wife, now in her true form as Yamanba, ran and ran, carrying the tub.

After a while, though Yamanba was strong, she seemed to get tired. She found a nice rock under a tree, sat down, and took a rest.

That gave the man a chance to escape. He reached for a branch above him and climbed out of the tub into the tree, kicking the lid back into place on the tub.

Yamanba didn't notice that he was gone. When she picked up the tub again she said, "Oh, after a nice rest, the tub feels lighter. Good. Good."

When Yamanba got back to her mountain home and opened the lid to show her souvenir to her neighbors, she found that the man had run away. She hurried after him. But the man had run down the mountain, and hid himself in a grassy field full of sweet-flag and mugwort.

Yamanba came after him. "I smell him. His smell is coming from this way."

As she went through the field, the sharp leaves of sweet-flag poked her eyes. She could not see. Still, she followed him by smell.

But it is said that supernatural creatures don't like the smell of mugwort. "I don't like this smell," said Yamanba. She couldn't come any closer. She gave up and went back to her mountain.

The man barely escaped with his life and went back to his home. After that, he hung mugwort and sweet rushes under the eaves of his house to protect him from Yamanba.

It was on May 5. Even today, village people hang sweet-flag leaves and mugwort from their house eaves on May 5 to ward off evil.

Oshimai!

CLOTHES BLEACHED IN THE MOONLIGHT

*O*nce upon a time, there was a young woman. She was the only daughter of the village headman, so her marriage was arranged very carefully.

At the beginning, she liked her husband. He was a good man. But soon she found him annoying. She couldn't stand the sound he made when he chewed food. She couldn't stand how he dragged his sandals when he walked. Everything about him annoyed her; she couldn't help it. In the end, she couldn't stand even looking at his face.

But he was a handsome man. He worked hard from early morning till late at night. He was good to his in-laws, too. So, there was nothing about which she could complain to her parents. If she told them that she wanted a divorce, they would not forgive her.

It was hopeless.

After long thought, she decided to go to Basama in the mountains. This Basama lived on a mountain over a mountain over a mountain over a mountain. It was a hard journey.

When the wife got there, Basama was weaving.

The wife bowed her head without saying anything. Then she opened her mouth. "Well . . . ."

Before she could say anything more, Basama turned to her and looked her in the face. "Are you really sure about this?" she asked.

The wife nodded slowly.

Basama said, "All right then. Walk toward the west from here. Walk on and on until you find a tree covered with many silk caterpillars. These caterpillars will spin cocoons.

"Then, on a night with a beautiful full moon, go there and gather the cocoons.

"Then, on a night with a beautiful full moon, reel the silk off those cocoons.

"Then, on a night with a beautiful full moon, spin thread out of the silk.

"Then, on a night with a beautiful full moon, weave cloth with it.

"Then, on a night with a beautiful full moon, bleach the cloth in the moonlight.

Clothes Bleached in the Moonlight

"Then, on a night with a beautiful full moon, make it into a kimono for your husband. But remember. No one should know about it until you finish making the kimono. And when it is done, then, on a night with a beautiful full moon, help your husband to dress in the kimono."

That was what Basama taught the wife.

The wife walked toward the west right away and found a tree covered with many silk caterpillars.

She waited until they had spun cocoons. And, on a night with a beautiful full moon, she took the cocoons home. She counted nights on her fingers and waited.

Then, on a night with a beautiful full moon, she reeled the silk off these cocoons. She waited again.

And then, on a night with a beautiful full moon, she spun thread from the silk.

Then, on a night with a beautiful full moon, she wove it into cloth.

Then, on a night with a beautiful full moon, she bleached it in the moonlight.

Then, on a night with a beautiful full moon, she made it into a kimono for her husband.

Then, on a night with a beautiful full moon, she said to her husband, "I made you a kimono." She helped him into the kimono, lapping the right side over the left.

Her husband was very happy that his wife had made something for him. He didn't mind that it was white, like a burial gown. He didn't notice that she lapped the right side over the left, like a burial gown, instead of left-over-right as living people always wear their kimonos.

But as soon as he was dressed in this white silk kimono, he started for the door and went outside.

And he never returned.

The wife kept calm for a while, but her uneasiness grew and grew. She wanted to know what had become of him. She decided to go to Basama in the mountain again.

She went over a mountain, and over a mountain, and over a mountain and got to Basama's hut on the fourth mountain. Basama was weaving again.

The wife bowed her head again. "Well . . . ."

Before she could say anything more, Basama turned to her and asked, "Do you want to know?"

"Yes," the wife nodded.

Basama told her, "On a night with a beautiful full moon, wait at the Six Way Crossroad." The wife bowed again and went back home.

She counted. And on a night with a beautiful full moon, she went to the Six Way Crossroad at the edge of the village. The sun set, and the full moon rose from behind the mountain. With moonlight at his back, a man in a white kimono came toward her.

"Oh, is that my husband?" she wondered.

As she watched, the man came toward her.

It was hard to tell whether he could see her or not. Without looking at her, he just passed by her. As he passed, she could hear him chanting:

"By unwittingly wearing
"Clothes made by moonlight
"I am now in attendance
"On the god of night."

Oshimai!

PICKING MOUNTAIN PEARS

This story includes many traditional sound effect words, and lots of formulaic repetition. Although this may look foolish and boring on the printed page, it can be great fun for a live audience—particularly if you encourage them to say the sounds and repeats with you. You will be amazed at how quickly they learn their parts.

*O*nce upon a time, there lived a mother and her three sons. The mother became seriously sick. She couldn't even get up from her bed. Her sons cooked all kinds of food, hoping she would eat some. But she kept saying, "No, I don't want to eat that. No, I don't feel like it."

The sons were worried. If she did not eat anything, she would soon die. So they kept cooking, trying every new food. But the mother wouldn't eat. She didn't have any appetite. Each day she became thinner and thinner. They started to wonder how many more days she could live.

Then, suddenly, the mother said, "Ahh, I want to eat a mountain pear. That's what I want."

The first son, Taro, heard this and said, "I'll go and get some mountain pears."

So he went. He walked in a hurry, *zunga, zunga, zunga, zunga* [sound of trudging along].

On a huge rock at the foot of the mountain sat an old woman. She called out, "Hey, Taro. Where are you going?"

"I'm climbing the mountain to pick some mountain pears," he replied.

"I see, then I will tell you. On the way to the mountain, there is a bamboo bush. It will sing, 'Go, go, *saara-sara*' [sound of wind rustling the leaves], or 'Don't go, *saara-sara*.' If you hear 'Don't go, *saara-sara*,' I advise you, don't go.

"Next, you will hear a bird sing, 'Go, go, *ton-ton*' [sound of chirping], or 'Don't go, *ton-ton*.' If you hear 'Don't go, *ton-ton*,' I advise you, don't go.

"Next, you will see a waterfall. It will sing, 'Go, go, *do-don*' [sound of water falling], or 'Don't go, *do-don*.' If you hear 'Don't go, *do-don*,' I advise you, don't go," the old woman told him kindly.

But Taro was in such a hurry that he didn't listen. He kept climbing up the mountain, *zunga, zunga, zunga, zunga*.

He came to the bamboo bush. It sang, "Don't go, *saara-sara*. Don't go, *saara-sara*." But Taro was in such a hurry that he didn't hear it. He went, *zunga, zunga*.

He came to where the bird sang. It sang, "Don't go, *ton-ton*. Don't go, *ton-ton*." But Taro was in such a hurry that he didn't hear it. He went, *zunga, zunga*.

He came to the waterfall. It sang, "Don't go, *do-don*. Don't go, *do-don*." But Taro didn't hear it. He went, *zunga, zunga*.

Then he came to a big pear tree by a big swamp. The tree was full of fruit.

"Oh, these are the mountain pears. I will pick some." Taro was about to climb the tree when a small child emerged from behind the tree.

The child talked to Taro. "When you climb that tree, you have to chant, 'Grow, grow, *zun-zun*. Grow, grow, *zun-zun*.' See?"

"Oh, I see. If I chant that song, the pears will grow bigger and bigger," Taro thought. So he sang, "Grow, grow, *zun-zun*. Grow, grow, *zun-zun*." And he climbed the tree. "Grow, grow, *zun-zun*. Grow, grow, *zun-zun*"

However, it was not the tree or the fruits that grew. It was the small child that grew.

Every time Taro chanted, the child became bigger and bigger. It became huge and swallowed up Taro.

Meanwhile, at their house, the family were waiting for Taro. But he never came back.

The second son, Jiro, said, "I'll go to pick the mountain pears." And off he went.

He hurried, *zunga, zunga, zunga, zunga*. At the foot of the mountain sat the old woman with white hair on a huge rock.

"Jiro, Jiro, where are you going?"

"I'm climbing the mountain to pick some mountain pears," Jiro replied. He hurried on his way.

But she called after him, "Wait, wait! I'll tell you. On the way to the mountain, there is a bamboo bush. It will sing, 'Go, go, *saara-sara*,' or 'Don't go, *saara-sara*.' If you hear 'Don't go, *saara-sara*,' I advise you, don't go.

"Next, you will hear a bird sing, 'Go, go, *ton-ton*,' or 'Don't go, *ton-ton*.' If you hear 'Don't go, *ton-ton*,' I advise you, don't go.

"Next, you will see a waterfall. It will sing, 'Go, go, *do-don*,' or 'Don't go, *do-don*.' If you hear 'Don't go, *do-don*,' I advise you, don't go," the old woman told him kindly.

But Jiro was in such a hurry, too. He kept climbing up the mountain, *zunga, zunga, zunga, zunga.*

He came to the bamboo bush. It sang, "Don't go, *saara-sara.* Don't go, *saara-sara.*" But Jiro was in such a hurry that he didn't hear it. He went, *zunga, zunga.*

He came to where the bird sang. It sang, "Don't go, *ton-ton.* Don't go, *ton-ton.*" But Jiro was in such a hurry that he didn't hear it. He went, *zunga, zunga.*

He came to the waterfall. It sang, "Don't go, *do-don.* Don't go, *do-don.*" But Jiro didn't hear it. He went, *zunga, zunga.*

Then he came to the big pear tree by the big swamp. "Oh, these fruits look good." Jiro was about to climb the tree when a small child appeared.

The child told Jiro, "When you climb that tree, you have to chant, 'Grow, grow, *zun-zun.*' See?"

So Jiro sang, "Grow, grow, *zun-zun.* Grow, grow, *zun-zun,*" as he climbed the tree.

The child started to grow. Every time Jiro sang, the child became larger and larger. Finally, he swallowed up Jiro.

Meanwhile, at their house, the family were waiting for Taro and Jiro. But neither of them came back. The third son, Saburo, decided to go. And off he went.

He hurried, *zunga, zunga, zunga, zunga.* On the huge rock at the foot of the mountain sat the old woman with white hair. "Saburo, Saburo, where are you going?"

"I'm climbing the mountain to pick some mountain pears," Saburo replied.

"Oh, I see. Then I'll tell you. On the way to the mountain, there is a bamboo bush. It will sing, 'Go, go, *saara-sara,*' or 'Don't go, *saara-sara.*' If you hear 'Don't go, *saara-sara,*' I advise you, don't go."

"Oh, I see," Saburo replied. He was listening to the woman well.

The woman continued, "Next, you will hear a bird sing, 'Go, go, *ton-ton,*' or 'Don't go, *ton-ton.*' If you hear 'Don't go, *ton-ton,*' I advise you, don't go."

Next, you will see a waterfall. It will sing, 'Go, go, *do-don,*' or 'Don't go, *do-don.*' If you hear 'Don't go, *do-don,*' I advise you, don't go," the old woman told him kindly.

"Oh, I see."

Because Saburo was listening to her very carefully, the old woman added, "Here, I have this sword. It might be useful for you, so take it with you. And I warn you, at the pear tree, a small child will show up and tell you to say, 'Grow, grow, *zun-zun.*' But you had better not listen to him." She even taught this.

Saburo thanked her and climbed the mountain, *zunga, zunga, zunga, zunga.*

After a while, he came to the bamboo bush. It sang, "Don't go, *saara-sara.* Don't go, *saara-sara.*"

Saburo heard this. "Aha! I should not go now." He decided to take a rest. He lay down there and took a nap.

When he woke up, the bamboo bush was singing, "Go, go, *saara-sara*. Go, go, *saara-sara*."

"Aha! 'Go, go, *saara-sara*.' I should go now," he said and hurried, *zunga, zunga*.

Soon he heard a bird sing, "Don't go, *ton-ton*. Don't go, *ton-ton*."

"Oh, the bird is singing, 'Don't go, *ton-ton*.' I should take another rest here." Saburo took a nap again.

When he woke up, the bird was singing, "Go, go, *ton-ton*. Go, go, *ton-ton*." Saburo hurried on his way again, *zunga, zunga, zunga, zunga*.

Then, he came to the waterfall. It sang, "Don't go, *do-don*. Don't go, *do-don*."

"Aha! I should take a rest again!" Saburo took a nap once more. When he woke up, he heard, "Go, go, *do-don*. Go, go, *do-don*."

"Good. Now I can go." He went on and on, *zunga, zunga, zunga, zunga*.

He came to the big pear tree by the swamp. The tree was full of fruit. Saburo was about to climb up the tree when the small child appeared. "When you climb this tree, you should say, 'Grow, grow, *zun-zun*. Grow, grow, *zun-zun*.' See?" said the child.

"Oh, really?" Saburo pretended to listen.

He thought, "That old woman taught me not to take this boy's advice. Maybe I should say the opposite."

"Don't grow, *zun zun*. Don't grow, *zun zun*," he chanted.

As he climbed the tree, he kept singing, "Don't grow, *zun zun*." When he looked down, he found that the child had shrunk to bean-size.

Saburo now felt safe and began to pick pears. He put them in his jacket and sleeves. "There are plenty here. There are plenty over there, too." He moved to the swamp side of the tree.

Then from that swamp, a huge monster rose up. It opened its mouth wide in order to swallow him.

Saburo remembered the sword the woman had given to him. He knew it was time to use it. He threw the sword into the monster's mouth. The monster swallowed it. It cut open the monster's belly. And out popped Taro and Jiro!

The three brothers were very happy. They picked many mountain pears and went back home together.

The mountain pears pleased their mother very much. She enjoyed eating them.

The next day, she was already up from her bed.

Oshimai!

OLD WOMAN'S SKIN

*O*nce upon a time, there was a man and woman who were happily married. When she had a baby girl, their happiness was even greater. Then I don't know what went wrong, but the wife became sick and soon passed away. The man couldn't raise his daughter properly all by himself. So he married another woman.

In the beginning, this stepmother treated the girl with love. But soon she had her own baby. She became more attached to her own child. And she began to be hard on the girl. Though the girl was still very young, she handed the girl all the kimonos to wash. "Go to the river and wash them all," the stepmother told the girl.

The girl went to the river and washed them all. When she returned home with the laundry, her stepmother said, "What a nasty job you have done! All the neckbands are still dirty. Go back and wash them again."

The girl went back to the river, and washed the neckbands of all the kimonos. She washed this kimono and that kimono. She washed every neckband clean, and went back home. Then, her stepmother said, "What a careless job you have done! The bottom hems are all still dirty."

The girl went back to the river again, and washed the bottoms of all the kimonos, this kimono and that kimono. Then she went back home with the laundry. But her stepmother said, "Why, all the kimono cuffs are still dirty."

The girl went back to the river a fourth time. When she washed them and returned home, her stepmother said, "All the armholes are still dirty."

Then the girl went back to the river again and washed them all.

She learned how to get them completely clean.

She had to cook rice, too. When she washed the rice hard, her stepmother scolded her that she was crushing the grains. When she washed the rice gently, her stepmother scolded her that the rice still smelled of rice bran. She had to use rowan wood for the fire. Rowan is a very hard wet wood, difficult to make fire with. So, though she tried hard, only smoke came out of the wood. And even when she finally made a fire, it seemed to go out after just a minute.

Her stepmother always had something to complain about. Today's rice is too soft. Today's rice is too hard. Today's rice is undercooked. Today's rice is not sticky enough. The girl cooked rice every day as her stepmother scolded her.

Trying hard, she became a skilled cook.

She had to wash dishes, too. When she washed the inside of a pot clean, her stepmother scolded her that the bottom was still dirty. When she washed the bottom, her stepmother scolded her that there was some rice on the side of the pot. When she washed the rice bowls and plates hard, her stepmother scolded her that she would chip the rims. In those days, people used a straw ball for a sponge. The stepmother scolded that she used too many straws to make a ball.

But in this way, the girl became skillful.

At meals, she was scolded that she hadn't set the table right, or she hadn't served the food correctly. Her stepmother slapped her hand, saying she wasn't holding her chopsticks or bowl properly. She was scolded that she wasn't sitting right, or that she ate too slowly.

But in this way, she learned manners.

When she sewed, she was scolded that her stitches were too big, too small, or not straight. She was scolded that she used too much margin or too little margin. She was scolded that she couldn't tell the difference between warps and woofs. When she put on a patch, she was scolded that it was too big. When she made it small, she was scolded that it would not cover the hole.

But in this way, she learned how to sew.

She was scolded when she cleaned the house. She was scolded that she didn't dust off the frame or doorsill properly. Her stepmother found dust in the corner of the room, or a cobweb at the ceiling. She was scolded that she had wrung out a wet cloth too tight, or too softly.

But in this way, she learned how to clean. She swept carefully every corner. When she slid a door open, she dusted the sill. She dusted off the frame, too. She wiped with a damp cloth not only the floor but also the wooden doors. She even wiped the bamboo stick on which pots hung over the hearth. She learned all these details as her stepmother scolded her.

When you weave, you first stretch long warp threads on the loom. The girl was scolded that she stretched them too tight or too loose. Her stepmother cut off the warp, saying the weft cross-threads were not going evenly, or the pattern did not match. Then the girl had to start all over again. She had to unsew a kimono, wash it, and starch it on a wooden board or with a bamboo tool. Again, she was scolded that she starched one side too thick, and the other side too thin.

Everything she did, she was scolded and slapped. She was crying all the time. But she listened to her stepmother obediently and learned all kinds of work and proper manners. Eventually she learned it so well that she could do everything without her stepmother scolding her.

Now her stepmother had nothing to scold her about. It made the stepmother hate the girl even worse. One day, while the girl was washing clothes in the river, the stepmother pushed her from behind and she fell into the river!

She was floating in the river unconscious. Basama found her, helped her out of the river, and listened to her story.

"You will be killed if you stay with your stepmother. Why don't you stay with me until you become stronger again?" asked Basama. Basama brought her to her house on the mountain. Until the girl became well, she stayed with the old woman.

Then one day, Basama said, "It will not get you anywhere if you stay here any longer. Why don't you go to a town and find a job? But it is dangerous for a young girl like you to go to a town alone. I have a disguise here. It is called Old Woman's Skin. If you put this on, even a young girl like you will look like an old woman."

She put the skin on the girl, and taught her how to get to the town. The girl thanked Basama and started off.

She walked on and on but it became dark before she got to the town. When it became dark, lots of gamblers gathered by the road and started gambling. She had to walk past that place. The gamblers saw her, but they said, "Oh, it's just an old grandma." They let her go by.

Finally she reached the town. She went to a big mansion. "I want to be a rice cooking woman. Could you hire me, please?" she asked.

It happened that their rice cooking woman had just quit her job, so the girl was hired. They gave her a little shed as her room. When it rained, water leaked in the roof. When the wind blew, it came in. But at least she had her own place.

During the day, she wore the Old Woman's Skin and worked from morning till night. She cooked rice, cleaned the house, went on errands, and did all kinds of other chores. At night, after the family and all the other servants took a bath, she took the last bath. The water in the hot tub was tepid and as low as her knees, and it was thick with dirt. But after she took the bath, she didn't have to put the Old Woman's Skin on, because nobody would see her. She went back to her room carrying the skin. She lit a lamp with the little oil she was given and sewed her own things, or wrote something. She had learned from her own mother how to write poetry and play *koto* (large stringed instrument). But of course, there was no koto to play. So the only thing she could enjoy was jotting down something on a scrap of paper or a board she found somewhere.

One night, after everybody else had taken a bath, she took her bath. Then without wearing the skin, she was writing something in her room.

The second son of the family happened to come home late after he had enjoyed his night life. He saw a light coming from the shed room. "What? The basama in the shed room still has a light on."

He peeked in. There was no basama. Instead, there was a beautiful lady writing something. At a glance, the son fell in love.

"Oh, what a beautiful lady! I would like to marry a lady like her. But that shed room is the room of the rice cooking woman. What is the relationship between the lady and the basama? Perhaps she is an enchantress."

So, he couldn't tell what he saw to his mother and father. He just kept thinking, "I want to see her once more." So he often peeked in the shed room. But he only found the basama in there.

He pined, "I want to see her once more. I've got to see her once more." He kept on thinking, and became sick. He couldn't get out of his bed.

His mother and father were worried. They asked many doctors and medicine men. But he didn't get any better.

One day, there came a shaman. They invited him in and asked him to see their son. He looked at their second son and then told them, "It seems that your son has a love sickness. I want to talk to him alone, so please leave us."

When he was alone with the second son the shaman told him, "You know, you will die if you just keep lying here. If you have a woman in your mind, please tell me her name. I will talk to your parents. I will see to it that everything goes well for you."

But the second son wouldn't tell.

"Then, you don't have to tell her name. Can you just tell me where she lives?"

The second son whispered in a very faint voice, "She lives in this household."

The shaman told his mother and father, "It seems your son is deeply in love with somebody who works in this house. Send every woman to him with a cup of tea, and see whose tea he drinks. The woman whose tea he drinks is the one he loves. Let them get married, and he will be fine again."

His mother and father said, "There are many women working in this house. Maybe one of them is the beautiful woman he likes. Well, if that's so, that is fine with us."

Each woman was given a tray with a cup of tea and some sweets. They were sent to the second son one by one. "Please have some tea," they offered to the son lying in his bed, but he didn't drink any of it.

His parents thought, "Every woman in the family brought tea to him. He didn't take any. Maybe she is not the one in this house."

Then someone said, "Well, she is not young, but that rice cooking basama is also a woman."

"It's impossible that she could be the one!" they thought. "But it's true that she is a woman . . . . Basama, take a cup of tea to him."

So, the basama brought tea to him, and the second son drank it.

His mother and father were very surprised. "Oh, no! Of all women, he wants to marry this old rice cooking woman. But we can't let him marry her."

At that, the second son became ill again. He couldn't even eat. He became thinner and thinner every day. It looked as if he would die within one or two days.

His mother and father said, "We have no choice. He will be marrying the rice cooking basama." They called for her, and sent her to their second son.

Right before she went into his room, she took off her Old Woman's Skin disguise.

The second son was so happy to see her. "I want to marry you," he said to her.

He introduced the beautiful young woman to his parents. They were very surprised. "Well, if she is indeed his age, there is no problem. He can marry her." So they were married.

Soon, their first son and the last son got married, too. Then there arose the question of who would inherit the house.

The father said, "It doesn't really matter to me which one of my sons will inherit the house. What matters is the wife. If the wife is skillful, the house will prosper. In order to prosper, it's important to have a smart wife. Let's compare their wives and decide."

All three wives were called together, and the competition began.

First, they had to wash a kimono. The wife of the second son knew how to wash a kimono, thanks to the strict stepmother. She washed the neckband, the bottom hem, the cuffs, and the armholes thoroughly. When she finished, her mother-in-law checked the kimono and said, "As for laundry, the wife of the second son is the best."

Then, it was sewing. Each of them had to sew a kimono for her husband. The wife of the second son had learned sewing from the strict stepmother who had insisted on making even stitches and matching the pattern. Thanks to that, she could make a perfect kimono for her husband. It was stitched beautifully, and there was no wrinkle. The mother-in-law said, "As for sewing, the wife of the second son is the best."

Then, it was cooking rice. The wife of the second son used to cook rice with difficult rowan wood. So with better wood, she cooked rice as quick as a wink. She was also the best in weaving, composing a poem, writing, and everything else.

So it was decided that the second son would inherit the house. The second son and his wife lived happily ever after.

Oshimai!

PART 6

STORIES OF SUPER-
NATURAL CREATURES

Natural tanuki

*I*n Japanese folktales, Fox and Tanuki are the most famous shape-changing animals. They often transform themselves without any magic ritual—although Fox sometimes puts a leaf on his head and turns a somersault, landing on his feet in the new shape. They must concentrate hard in order to maintain their transformed shape. If they become confused or distracted or hurt, their natural shape returns one body part at a time, usually tail first.

Translators sometimes say "raccoon dog" or "badger" for tanuki, but this oriental animal is neither dog nor badger (see appendix A). Tanuki is tanuki.

There is a saying: "Fox changes seven times, Tanuki eight." Although Tanuki can change into more different things than Fox, he is not as clever and he changes himself into simpler things. While Fox is sometimes vengeful, Tanuki is foolish and usually good-natured. He likes to drink sake and drum on his belly.

THE MOON STICKS OUT ITS TONGUE

Amado Bridge is west of Fukushima City. Many tanuki used to live there.

One evening, two men from a village were walking near the Amado Bridge.

From the mountains a beautiful full moon rose up, so they admired it. Then a second moon rose up near a pine tree!

"Oh, we should admire this moon, too," said the men, but they knew it must be a tanuki. So they added, "It usually sticks out its tongue when we praise it. Will that happen this time?"

They admired one moon and then the other moon.

"Which moon will stick out its tongue?"

The moon by the pine tree stuck out its tongue. The two men picked up some mud and threw it at the second moon. And it disappeared.

Oshimai!

SPOOKY TANUKI MUSIC

*O*nce upon a time, there was a temple deep, deep in the mountains. Every night the temple's priest was haunted by spooky noises. He couldn't bear it, and he resigned.

The next priest was a jolly man. "Spooky or not, it's better to hear something than no sound at all. Well, what kind of noise will it be?"

The new priest waited for evening to fall. He sat in the middle of the main hall and finished his evening prayer. Then he kept sitting there.

After midnight it started. From the mountain behind the temple came a deep thumping sound: *Po-n!*

"Oh, I heard that strange noise! But just one! Well, why did it stop?" he wondered. Then, from the other direction, came a light tapping sound: *Poko, poko.* "I hear it," said the priest.

Po-n, poko, poko. Po-n, poko, poko.

From here, *Po-n!*

From there, *Po-n!*

From over there, *Poko, poko, poko, poko.*

The sounds became louder and louder. They were coming closer and closer to the temple.

Po-n, poko, poko.

The priest started to enjoy it. When he heard *po-n*, he rang his prayer gong: *Chi-n!* When he heard *poko, poko*, he beat his wood block: *poku, poku.*

Po-n, chi-n! Poko, poko, poku, poku!

Po-n, chi-n! Poko, poko, poku, poku!

It seemed like the noise makers were gathering in the temple garden.

Po-n, chi-n! Poko, poko, poku, poku!

Po-n, chi-n! Poko, poko, poku, poku!

Po-n, chi-n! Poko, poko, poku, poku!

Po-n, chi-n! Poko, poko, poku, poku!

It was such fun.

The priest got more and more excited. "What is making this sound?" he wondered. "I will see what it is."

The priest stopped ringing his gong and moved quietly toward the window. When he looked out, those who were in the temple garden scattered away toward the mountain. Maybe it's because the priest stopped his part, or maybe it's because they noticed him opening the window. Anyway, the next evening the priest opened the window a little in advance and waited. After midnight, he heard the sound again: *Po-n, poko, poko.* It sounded like more and more noises were gathering.

Po-n, poko, poko.

Po-n, poko, poko.

Po-n, poko, poko.

More and more were gathering in the temple garden.

The priest looked. They were a group of tanuki.

Folktale tanuki

"Very well. I will join in." But then he thought, "I have to stop my gong and wood block if I want to see them. If I stop, they might run away again like yesterday. Tonight, instead of gong and wood block, I will use my belly."

So, at *Po-n* from the garden, he thumped his belly: *Becha.* At *Poko, poko* from the garden, he tapped his belly: *Pita, pita.*

Po-n. Becha.

Poko, poko. Pita, pita.

Po-n, becha. Poko, poko, pita, pita.

Po-n, becha, poko, poko, pita, pita.

Po-n, becha, poko, poko, pita, pita.

It was such fun.

Po-n, becha, poko, poko, pita, pita.

Po-n, becha, poko, poko, pita, pita.

The Tanuki were all enjoying it very much, too.

But after a while, everyone's bellies became red and started to hurt. In the end, they were all rubbing their bellies.

"This is very much fun," the priest told the tanuki, "but we can't do this every night. If we do, our bellies might burst. Why don't we do it only on the night of a full moon?"

He wasn't sure if they understood him. Without saying anything, the tanuki just went back to the mountain.

But he didn't hear anything the next night, and the next night, and the next.

On the next full moon night, the priest waited eagerly. From the mountain, he heard it.

Po-n.

Poko, poko.

Po-n, poko, poko.

Po-n, poko, poko.

They were gathering in the garden. The priest went out to the garden, too. When the tanuki went *Po-n*, the priest went *Becha*. When they went *Poko, poko*, he went *Pita, pita*. And from then on, on full moon nights, the villagers could hear from the temple:

Po-n, becha, poko, poko, pita, pita.

Po-n, becha, poko, poko, pita, pita.

Oshimai!

TANUKI WHO TURNED INTO A DIE

*O*nce upon a time, there was an old man. When he was working in the mountains, he heard a cry. It was a little tanuki, caught in a snare. The old man freed him.

That night, the father tanuki came to the old man and said, "Thank you very much for saving my son. I would like to repay you. But I'm not so good at turning into things. The only thing I can become is a die. But sir, you can take me to a gambling house. I will give you the number you ask for."

"Really? That will be nice. But in a dice game, do you know which numbers are Cho and which are Han?" asked the old man.

"No."

"When we call *Han* (half) we mean an odd number like one, three, and five. When we call *Cho* (a pair) we mean two, four, and six."

"I see. One, three and five are Han. Two, four, and six are Cho. I got it."

Tanuki turned into a die. And with that die in his hand, the old man went to a gambling house. He approached the dice thrower and changed one of the two dice for his tanuki die.

The dice thrower put the two dice into a bowl and said, "Everyone ready? Ready?"

He shook the bowl, rattling the dice. Tanuki in that bowl bumped here and there. His eyes were rolling. But he tried hard not to miss what the old man was going to say.

"Han!"

Tanuki heard him.

"Well . . . Han, it's one, three, and five. Then, I will give him one."

Tanuki gave one. The rattler opened the bowl and said,

"A pair of ones—Cho!"

Tanuki wondered, "Why? Old man said one is Han. But did I hear it wrong?"

Tanuki didn't know that in dice gambling, you must add the numbers of the two dice. If the total is odd (three, five, etc.), it is Han. If the total is even (two, four, etc.) it is Cho. One plus one is two. So it is Cho. But Tanuki didn't know arithmetic. He just thought if he gave one, it would be Han.

"If one isn't Han, then, two, four, and six must be Han," Tanuki thought.

On the next throw, he heard the old man say, "Cho!" Tanuki thought he should give four.

"Four and three," said the rattler. "Han!"

Tanuki didn't know he had to add the numbers on two dice, he didn't know four plus three is seven, he didn't know which was odd or even. He got so confused.

"What is Han? What is Cho?" He was so puzzled that he couldn't keep his die shape. His tail popped out. The gamblers shouted in surprise.

The shouting scared Tanuki so much that he returned to his natural Tanuki shape. The gamblers began to chase after him.

The old man put back the original die and quietly slipped away.

Oshimai!

THE FOX BARBER

*O*nce upon a time, in the mountains near a village there lived a fox who was very good at tricking people. Once he stole all the treats a man was taking home from a wedding party. Another man, who thought he had caught a big fish, found only a log when he got home. Fox tricked the villagers in many ways.

But there was one man who said, "That fox can't fool me. I will detect him and punish him." So he went into the mountains, hid behind a tree, and waited very still.

Then Fox came walking through the woods. "Ah, here he comes," the man thought and kept watching.

Fox put a leaf on his head and did a somersault. When he landed on his feet, he was a beautiful young lady!

"Wow! She is so beautiful. But I was watching. She is really a fox. I saw how he did it." He kept watching.

The young lady picked up a thick piece of log lying nearby and flipped it over. It became a baby.

Then she picked up chunks of horse dung and wrapped them in a big butterbur leaf. When she flipped it over, it became a box of botamochi cakes in a carrying cloth. She started walking, swishing the silken skirts of her kimono *shanari, shanari, shanari, shanari.* She walked toward the village with the baby in her arms, carrying the box of botamochi.

"All right. I will follow her and see whom she is going to trick," the man thought and followed the woman.

She kept on walking, *shanari, shanari, shanari, shanari.* She didn't seem to notice that someone was following her.

At the very edge of the village lived an elderly couple. The young lady went to their house and slid the door open. "Hello, I have come back!" she called, and entered the house.

"Oh, it's nice of you to visit us," said the old folks.

"Let me hold my grandchild!" The old man took the baby.

"Oh, you brought us botamochi. Thank you!" The old woman unwrapped the box of cakes.

The watching man went around the house and peeped in through a knothole. "Stupid people! They don't know that is a fox. They think that is their married daughter. I will show them that she is a fake." He kept on peeping in.

The old man and old woman took turns holding the baby. Then they decided to eat the botamochi. The woman took one on her plate and was about to put it into her mouth.

"That botamochi is horse dung!" the man yelled in a loud voice. He slid the door open and hurried into the house.

The old woman was surprised. "Who on earth are you?"

The man explained, "I saw what happened. You think she is your daughter, but she is not. I was watching it all from behind a tree. A fox put a leaf on his head and became a woman. He flipped over a log that became a baby. And that botamochi is horse dung. Don't eat it."

The old woman said, "What are you saying? You shouldn't call my precious daughter a fox. This baby isn't a log either, smiling like an angel. My daughter made this botamochi for us. Why do you say it is horse dung? You are such a disgusting man!"

But the man insisted. "She is a fox. I saw it with my own eyes. You are being fooled." Then he had an idea. "You know what? It is said that a fox reveals its true form when you hold it in smoke. I will prove to you now that she is a fox."

He wound a rope round and round their daughter and hung her, head-down, from the rafters. Then he started building a big fire in their hearth.

The elders shrieked, "No! Please stop! What are you doing to our daughter? Stop it, please."

"You will see the truth soon. Just wait and watch!" Saying so, the man hung the young woman right over the fire. Smoke curled around her.

But soon she died, without revealing her fox-self.

"What?" The man let her down in a hurry.

The old man and woman protested, "Why did you do this to our daughter? Now, what are you going to do about it?"

The man became worried. "Well, I was sure I saw a fox turn into a woman. But did I make a mistake somewhere?" He apologized to them. "I'm sorry. Somehow I made a mistake. I'm really sorry. But I was sure it was a fox."

They were very upset. "Oh, what have you done?" they yelled in a loud voice. They hit him and punched him.

While they were making a big scene, a priest came by. "What's the matter? What is this all about?"

The priest came into the house. The old people explained to him what had happened. "This man did this to our precious daughter. We are so angry at him. And for that, we are now hitting him."

The priest listened and said to the man, "I see. I see. It's your fault. You can't smoke someone's daughter over the hearth. It is not surprising that she is dead. Do you know how much she suffered? Can you imagine her pain?"

"I'm so sorry." All he could do was bow down low and apologize. Still, inside him, he was wondering, "Something is wrong. Something is wrong."

But there lay their daughter in front of him. And she was dead. He had no choice but to apologize. "I'm so sorry." He kept bowing his head.

The priest said to the old man and woman, "Your daughter is dead, and there is nothing we can do to bring her back. Even if you beat him to death, your daughter will never come to life. I want you to trust this man to me. I want to train him, and make him a monk. Then, he can pray for your daughter as long as he lives. What do you think about that?"

They said, "That's right. Our daughter will never come to life, even if we beat him to death. Please make him a monk and make him pray for our daughter."

Then, the priest told the man, "Did you hear that? They have trusted you to me. Why don't you become a monk?"

"Yes, whatever you say," replied the man.

"Very well. I'm glad you agreed. But you can't be a monk with your hair long. I will shave your head now. My razor isn't sharp. It might hurt a little bit. But you must endure the pain. Think of their daughter, how much she suffered from being smoked over the hearth. Then you can endure any pain," scolded the priest.

"Yes." The man knelt on the floor in front of the priest.

The priest took out his razor. *Jori* [sound of dull razor scraping the man's head].

"Ouch!"

"Think of their daughter. How much she suffered over the hearth. You couldn't say that this hurts," said the priest.

"That's true," thought the man. He tried to bear the pain.

Jori.

"Ouch!!" he cried, but the priest said, "Think of their daughter."

The man thought, "Their daughter suffered to death. Compared to that, this is just my hair." He tried to endure the pain.

Jori.

The razor seemed to scrape his scalp roughly.

Jori.

"Oh, it feels like something is biting my head. Not just cutting my hair, but biting my scalp." Yet he sat there and tried to bear the pain with his eyes closed.

Then from afar, he heard villagers calling. "What are you doing? With foxes around you, why are you kneeling on the ground?"

Startled, he opened his eyes. He saw many foxes running away from him.

Villagers came running to help him. And they asked the man, "Why were you letting the foxes bite your head?"

Oshimai!

FOX TEAKETTLE

Unlike European and North American foxes, Japanese foxes have golden brown fur. Cartoons often show them as bright yellow!

Once upon a time, there was an old junk man who went from house to house collecting things that people didn't need any more. He fixed the things or cleaned them, then sold them to other people.

One day when he was at home, he heard a loud yelp from the mountain behind his house. He leaped up in surprise and went to investigate. A little fox cub had his leg caught in a trap which somebody had set. The old man felt pity, so he helped the fox cub out of the trap.

The fox cub was so grateful. But then it ran off and was gone behind a bush.

The next day, a female fox came to the man. "Thank you very much for yesterday, for saving my baby. I can't thank you enough. But to show you how much we appreciate your kindness, I'm going to turn myself into a teakettle. Take me to town and sell me to the priest or somebody who would buy me," said Fox.

"No, no, I didn't rescue the little fox to get something in return. Don't worry about it," said the old man.

But Fox put a leaf on her head and did a somersault. She became a shiny gold teakettle, not an everyday kettle but the kind used to heat water for the tea ceremony.

"You have turned into a really a splendid teakettle! I'll try taking you to the priest," said the old man.

He put that gold teakettle in his back-basket and carried it down to the town.

He walked around the town, calling, "Teakettle! Teakettle! A golden teakettle!!"

People on the street looked into his basket.

"Oh my. What a splendid teakettle!"

"This is a shiny beauty! But such a wonderful teakettle must be expensive. It is too good to sit in my house."

They just looked at it, nobody wanting to buy. The old man walked on to the temple. "Priest, Priest. I happened to have a gold teakettle. Would you buy it?" asked the man.

"Let me see." The priest held it and looked. "Yes, this is a beautiful teakettle, a wonderful thing. All right, I'll take it."

The priest paid a lot of money to the old junk man, who went home happily.

The priest was happy, too. "This really is a beautiful teakettle. The color is hard to name. Golden? Or should I call it the color of a fox? Anyway, it's a beautiful color. A wonderful teakettle, indeed!"

He stared at it from this side and from that side, from the top and from the bottom. Being stared at so long, Fox felt embarrassed. She blushed and turned red.

The priest was amazed, "Well, well. It becomes reddish with sunset light. What a beautiful teakettle this is!" Then he thought, "This looks fine. But you never know who used it before. I should have it washed thoroughly first." He called a young apprentice. "Take this teakettle to the well and wash it," he ordered.

So the apprentice took it to the well. This young man loved singing. He hummed all the way to the well. He hummed while he drew water. He hummed as he started rubbing the teakettle.

When spring comes,
Plum, peach, and cherry trees,
They all bloom.

Sometimes he forgot to rub. But he didn't forget humming.

Fox thought, "This is an interesting song. I want to listen to it more carefully." So she pricked up her ear.

A furry ear stuck out from the teakettle.

The apprentice was so surprised. "Priest, Priest! This teakettle has an ear!!" he yelled.

But the priest inside the temple scolded the apprentice, "Of course! Every teakettle has an ear."

"Oh, I see," thought the apprentice.

Well, a Japanese teakettle has a short skirt around its base. It is called a "wing" or sometimes, an "ear." The priest thought this was the kind of "ear" the apprentice was describing.

The apprentice started polishing it again. He rubbed it here. Rubbed it there. Humming, he rubbed.

> When summer comes,
> Plum, peach, and cherry trees,
> They all bear fruits.

He rubbed all over.

The fox was ticklish. She could not help giggling.

The apprentice was so surprised. "Priest, Priest! This teakettle makes a sound!" he yelled.

But the priest inside the temple scolded him. "Of course! A good teakettle, when it is filled with water, makes a ringing sound."

"Oh, I see."

The apprentice started polishing the kettle again, this time upside-down. He was rubbing its bottom. As he rubbed, he hummed.

> When autumn comes,
> Plum, peach, and cherry trees,
> They all have fallen leaves.

He rubbed the bottom, and Fox couldn't help wiggling.

The apprentice was so surprised. "Priest, Priest! This teakettle shakes its bottom!" he yelled.

But the priest inside the temple scolded him, "Of course! A good teakettle, when filled with water, makes a ringing sound. And at the same time, its bottom vibrates."

"Oh, I see."

The apprentice started polishing again. He rubbed and rubbed. He rubbed the kettle with all his might, humming.

> When winter comes,
> Plum, peach, and cherry trees,
> They all are covered with snow.

He rubbed and rubbed. He rubbed the same place over and over.

Fox became sore. "I wish this apprentice would move his hand a little." She tried to push his hand gently to another spot. Her paws came out of the teakettle.

The apprentice was so surprised. "Priest, Priest! This teakettle has hands!" he yelled.

The priest inside the temple scolded the apprentice. "Of course! How do you hold a teakettle if it doesn't have handles? Of course it should have handles. Now, don't be so slow. Hold that round handle and bring it inside."

"Yes, sir." The apprentice stopped rubbing, held the teakettle by the round handles and took it inside.

The priest looked at the beautifully washed teakettle. "My goodness, polishing made it look even more splendid. Now, I will set it in the alcove so everyone can admire it." In the morning and at night, he enjoyed its beauty.

One day, they learned that a great priest from the capital planned to visit the temple. The priest said, "Tomorrow, when the great priest comes here, I will make tea for him with this teakettle."

Fox, sitting solemnly in the alcove, overheard it and was surprised. "I suppose I have to stand being rubbed. But putting me on the fire? No! I can't bear it!"

That night, she jumped out the window and ran back to the mountain.

Oshimai!

A HOIN MONK AND A FOX

*O*nce upon a time, a young Hoin monk was testing himself by going on a pilgrimage in the mountains all alone, unarmed except for a big conch shell horn with which to scare bears. One sunny day he was walking along a mountain river when, in the tall grass, he saw something yellowish or brownish moving. He wondered what it was and pushed the tall grass aside to see.

There was a fox curled up in the grass, sleeping. Every time the wind blew, the fox's tail waved. But the fox was so soundly asleep that he didn't notice Hoin looking at him.

"What a stupid fox. Usually wild animals wake up just at the sound of human footsteps. What a stupid one this is. Oh, yes, I've got to play a trick on him."

He took out his big shell horn. He put it close to the fox's ear. He blew, *Buooo!!*

The fox, who had been sleeping peacefully, jumped up and fell in the river. *Bo chan!* [sound of a big splash].

Hoin couldn't help but laugh at the startled fox, "*Kera kera kera, Gya-haha!*"

He enjoyed a good laugh and went along on his way.

It was still before noon, and yet it started to get dark.

"What a short day we have today. I must find a safe place to stay for the night. Well, where shall I sleep?" the young monk wondered. He found a big hollow tree. "Yes, this is good shelter. I will take my rest here."

Just as he was getting in, there came a very soft sound from the distance.

Jaran, pon, chin . . . Jaran, pon, chin. He recognized the slow, somber sounds of a funeral procession.

"It is coming this way, but where is it going? Is there a temple around here?"

Far away, in the growing darkness, he saw many people walking toward him slowly banging drums and bells. *Jaran, pon, chin . . . Jaran, pon, chin.*

Next came the coffin. People carried it on their shoulders and walked very slowly. As they came closer and closer, the musical sounds became louder. *Jaran, pon, chin . . . Jaran, pon, chin.*

The procession came closer and closer.

"Is there a temple in this wilderness?" Hoin wondered.

Jaran, pon, chin . . . Jaran, pon, chin.

They came closer and closer. Finally they stopped at the hollow tree in which Hoin had planned to spend the night. They put down the coffin. Silently, they left—without the coffin.

"Oh, oh, why are they leaving the coffin here?" Hoin wondered.

But though he was still in training, he was a priest. It was his duty to sit up all night with the corpse and chant sutras for the dead person's soul.

"*Nanmaida, nanmaida,*" he chanted in the hollow of his tree. He leaned on the wall of the hollow.

"*Nanmaida, nanmaida,*" he grew drowsy. "Shall I sleep for a while?"

Kata!

Suddenly, a sharp noise came from the coffin.

Hoin was shocked awake and peeked out of his tree at the coffin.

The lid moved a little.

A very bony hand came out, trying to push the lid off.

Hoin was so astonished, he jumped out of his hiding hole. He hid behind the tree and peered around the trunk.

Gatan!

The coffin lid fell off with a big noise.

A bony body wearing white burial clothes stood up in the coffin. "Where is Hoin? Is he in the hollow of the tree?" The corpse went to the hole and searched.

Hoin was so astonished. "Ah, I was lucky to have got out of that hollow tree. Now, I'll hide in the branches." He climbed up the tree to the lowest branch, *suru suru suru!* [sound of fast climbing]. He sat and watched below.

"Where is Hoin? He was not in the hollow. Where is Hoin? Did he climb into the tree?" With those bony arms, the corpse started to climb slowly up the tree. *Zuru . . . Zuru . . . Zuru . . .* [sound of slow climbing]. "Where is Hoin? Is he on the lowest branch?"

Very astonished, Hoin climbed higher, *suru suru suru!* On the second lowest branch, he sat.

The corpse came up to the lowest branch and searched for him. "Where is Hoin? He is not on the lowest branch. Where is Hoin? Is he on the second lowest branch?"

Saying so, the corpse climbed further up. *Zuru . . . Zuru . . . Zuru . . . .*

Hoin was very astonished. Hurriedly, he climbed up, *suru suru suru* and sat on the third branch.

"Where is Hoin? Is he on the second branch?" The corpse looked for Hoin all over on the second branch. He looked through twigs and leaves. "Where is Hoin? He is not on the second branch. Where is Hoin? Is he on the third branch?"

The corpse climbed further up. *Zuru . . . Zuru . . . Zuru . . . .*

Hurriedly, Hoin went up, *suru suru suru,* and sat at the fourth branch.

The dead man came up to the third branch. "Where is Hoin? He is not on the third branch. Where is Hoin? Is he on the fourth branch?" He climbed again. *Zuru . . . Zuru . . . Zuru . . . .*

Hoin went up to the fifth branch. He went up to the sixth branch, seventh branch. Finally, he was on the top of the tree.

The corpse came up and up. He found Hoin on the thin twig at the top of the tree.

"I found Hoin. I'll catch Hoin." He came closer and closer. He tried to reach Hoin with his bony hands. His finger was reaching the foot of the Hoin monk.

Hoin pulled his foot up.

"I have almost got Hoin." The dead man raised his hand higher.

Hoin pulled up his other foot. Finally, he found that he couldn't go any further up.

"Hoin is there." The dead man reached higher.

Hoin tried to move up.

Suddenly the thin branch broke. Hoin fell down to the river below. *Bo chan!*

Suddenly, all around him, everything became as bright as midday.

Hoin heard somebody laugh, saying, "Hoin fell down. *Ken, ken, ken, ken!*" [sound of fox laughter].

Oshimai!

Kappas

In the distant past, Kappa may have been a powerful water god, but now he appears as a scary or foolish water monster of supernatural strength and healing magic. Kappas live in rivers, ponds, and other bodies of water. Traditional country people blamed kappas for unexplained drownings of people and farm animals, but respected the way they kept their promises.

Although kappas live under water, their favorite food is cucumbers. They risk coming on shore to raid farmers' gardens. Kappa roll (cucumber sushi—see Part 7) is named in their honor.

Kappas have strange stretchy bodies and oddly connected limbs. If you pull a kappa's right arm, its left arm gets shorter. If you pull its left arm, its right arm gets shorter. If you pull its leg, both arms get shorter! The traditional kappa toy (see Part 7) was made from a section of bamboo, but you can use a cardboard tube. Children are still surprised to see how it moves.

KAPPA'S PAPER

*O*nce upon a time, a farmer was washing his horse in a river. When he finished washing, he thought, "Now it's time to pull him out to the shore." But the horse didn't move an inch.

"What's wrong with him?" the farmer wondered.

He found something big hanging down from the horse's behind. "What is this?" It was the arm of a kappa. Kappa had grabbed the horse's behind and wouldn't let go.

The farmer pulled the horse hard, but Kappa wouldn't let go and his arm stretched longer. The farmer kept pulling, but it was no use. The farmer feared that Kappa wanted to drown his horse. Finally in desperation he gave the horse one last pull with all his might. At last, the horse came up on the shore. But Kappa's arm was still hanging down from the horse's behind.

You know, a kappa's arm is different from ours. It is one piece from its right hand to its left hand. So if Kappa's right hand was grabbing the horse's behind, both arms through to the left hand were hanging in one piece from the horse.

The farmer brought the horse back home, with Kappa's arms still hanging down. He couldn't pull them off. So he went to the temple and asked the priest for help.

The priest murmured some chants and pulled the arms off.

They decided to keep this rare thing in the main temple.

That night, somebody knocked on the temple door. It was Kappa.

"Please give me back my arms," asked Kappa.

"Well, it is no use giving you your arms. You can't put them back," said the priest.

"Yes, if you give them back to me, I can put them back on."

"Really? Then show me how you do it."

The priest gave the arms back to Kappa. Kappa squeezed the fingertips of one hand together. He poked the hand into a hole on one shoulder and pulled it out from a hole on the other shoulder. His arms were back where they belonged, and Kappa could move them again.

"Oh, thank you. I will never play a trick on people again," Kappa promised.

"Then you must sign a paper," said the priest.

"I can't write. Instead, I will stamp my handprint, with this hand as good as new."

The priest prepared black ink, dipped Kappa's hand in, and stamped his handprint on the paper.

They say that the paper is still in the temple.

Oshimai!

A KAPPA AND A FISH PEDDLER

*O*nce upon a time, there was a village fish peddler who caught fish to sell. Village people wouldn't pay much money for small river fish, so sometimes he went to the sea to catch big fish, brought them back to his village, and sold them.

One day as he was walking to the sea, he saw several naughty boys bullying a kappa they had caught. "Hey! You can't hurt a kappa like that," he scolded.

But the children replied, "This kappa does bad things when we're swimming, like pulling our leg. We think he's trying to drown us. So we'll kill him. Let's beat him to death." They beat the kappa with sticks, and made fun of him by pulling his legs and arms.

The fish peddler felt pity. "Then let me buy him from you. I'll pay you."

He bought the kappa. But before he released him, he warned, "You should go back home right away, or those boys might catch you again and hurt you. And from now on, never, never play tricks on human children. And never pull children's legs."

The money the fish peddler paid the boys was all he had that day. Now he had no money to buy bait. "It's no use going to the sea today." So he went back home. "Well, I guess I will just go to sleep early." He crawled into bed and fell asleep.

Early next morning, he heard a big thud in front of his house. "What is it?"

He went outside and saw a pile of fish at the door: sea bream, tuna and such. He thought, "Maybe the kappa I saved yesterday went to the sea and caught them for me."

That day, he sold those sea fish. "I made a lot of money today. Maybe I don't have to go fishing. I suppose I can go to sleep early again."

Early the next morning, he heard a big thud again. This time it was a pile of river fish.

Early each morning from then on, he heard a big thud and found a pile of fish, either river fish or sea fish, at the door. The fish peddler didn't have to catch fish any more. He sold them and made a lot of money.

But after three months or so, he realized something. "Oh, no. This is not right. If Kappa keeps bringing me fish, I will become lazy and hate working. I should ask him to stop it."

He went to the river and called, "Kappa! I don't want your fish any more. If you continue giving me fish, I'll become lazy. So don't bring me fish any more."

Then from the water he heard a voice. "Maybe that is the way human beings think. But we have our own way of doing things. Our reward is for one year. So you have to let me do it for one year."

So fish were delivered to the fish peddler every morning for one year. After one year, he thought, "Well, today is the last day."

But by then, he had indeed become lazy. He didn't want to go to the sea or to the river and fish. Besides, he already had saved a lot of money. "I will be well off for a while," he thought.

He lived in idleness. Within six months, however, his money was all gone. Finally one day, he thought, "Well, I suppose I have to go fishing again."

He went to the river. He cast his line into the water, and soon he caught something strange. "What is this?" he wondered. It looked like a very tiny kappa. "What? Are you a kappa?" he asked.

"I'm the god of the kappas," it said. "If you let me go, I will bring you rice that lasts for the rest of your life. So please let me go," the strange little creature begged.

The fish peddler thought for a while. "I saved a kappa once, but now I have no money. If I sell this strange thing to a showman, I'll be able to make some money." But the promise of a lifetime supply of rice sounded even better. "Very well, I'll let you go. But you have to keep your promise," he said to the god of the kappas.

"Of course. A god never breaks his promise. Even a common kappa always keeps his word. We know manners. Don't worry, just wait. Tomorrow morning, you will receive rice that lasts the rest of your life." Saying so, the god of the kappas disappeared into the water.

Next morning, the fish peddler found one bag of rice at his door.

"Huh, he promised rice that lasts for my lifetime but he brought only one bag. Is he going to bring me more after I finish this?" he wondered.

He ate the rice every day. Finally there was just one day's supply left. He cooked the rice and ate it, thinking, "Well, I finished all the rice that the god of the kappas brought me. I wonder if he will bring some more tomorrow morning?"

Suddenly, a big thunderbolt hit him and he was dead.

Kappas always keep their promises.

Oshimai!

A Kappa and a Fish Peddler

PART 7

FOOD, GAMES, AND CRAFTS

Making mochi

RECIPES

Gradually the ingredients for Japanese cooking are becoming more readily available in U.S. grocery stores and health food stores, but you may need to visit an oriental import store for some of them.

NOTE: See the "shopping list" at the end of this section for more details and descriptions of food terms you may not understand.

Mochi

Mochi is a traditional Japanese treat made of a special kind of rice, *mochi gome* (sweet/glutinous rice) which has an especially sticky texture. Making mochi the old fashioned way took many helpers and lots of time, but it was a part of joyous family events—comparable to old-fashioned American taffy pulls.

To make mochi the old fashioned way, one person uses a big wooden mallet to pound the steamed rice in a very heavy mortar carved from wood or stone, while a helper mixes and turns the hot rice by hand. When they have pounded the rice to a silky smooth dough, they divide it into portions or shape it around savory or sweet fillings.

Now, however, there is an electric appliance like a bread machine that can convert rice and water into fresh mochi without the work—or the fun. Ready-made mochi is also sold in confectionary shops and supermarkets in Japan and in some American cities with large Asian populations.

Fresh mochi is as chewy and elastic as the melted cheese on top of a pizza, but when it cools, it becomes hard and unappetizing. Fortunately it can be revived by warming it in hot broth, in a microwave oven, or—the best, traditional way—by slowly toasting it in the ashes of the hearth, as seen in several stories in this book.

If you can't buy mochi at import stores or borrow a mochi machine from a Japanese friend, following is a recipe for making a small batch (about twelve pieces).

CAUTION: Mochi sticks like superglue to anything dry. Handle it with WET hands and utensils, keep a wet cloth handy to moisten surfaces, and wipe up spills immediately.

Mochi

Ingredients:

1 cup *mochi gome* (sweet/glutinous rice)

water for rinsing and soaking

nylon net

Instructions:

1. *The night before,* wash the cup of mochi gome in at least three changes of water. Cover it with water and soak overnight. Drain.

2. Spread the soaked rice grains in a steamer basket lined with a layer of nylon net rinsed in water. Steam the rice over boiling water for 35–40 minutes, until all the rice is tender.

3. Thoroughly mash the rice in a heavy-duty electric mixer (the kind that can knead bread dough) or a food processor until it forms a smooth, elastic, very sticky mass. This will take at least 5 minutes.

4. With wet hands, pull off walnut-sized lumps of mochi and shape them into round cakes. They can be rolled in optional toppings such as toasted sesame seeds, ground nuts, or toasted soybean powder mixed with sugar. Or, set each piece on a square of *nori* (seaweed) and sprinkle with soy sauce. In addition to adding flavor, these toppings make the mochi easier to handle.

5. Serve at room temperature.

Mochi can be stored overnight at room temperature, or longer in the refrigerator. Keep it covered so it doesn't dry out. Reheat cold mochi briefly in a toaster oven or microwave oven. You can also toast plain mochi on a fork over a stove burner until it is crisp outside and molten inside.

Coconut Mochi

This chewy sweet is not a traditional Japanese recipe, but rather comes from third- and fourth-generation Japanese Americans. It is easy to make and very tasty, enjoyed even by children who are skeptical about exotic food.

Coconut *Mochi*

Ingredients:

    1 cup *mochiko* (sweet/glutinous rice flour)

    1 cup sugar

    1 cup unsweetened canned coconut milk

    ½ tsp coconut flavoring

    confectioner's (powdered) sugar

Instructions:

1. Preheat oven to 350°F.
2. Mix all ingredients thoroughly and pour into a well-greased pie plate or casserole. The mixture should be about ½ inch deep. Cover with casserole lid or aluminum foil.
3. Bake for 30 minutes.
4. Let cool, covered, for 15 minutes, then uncover and cool to room temperature. Cut the mochi in squares or scoop it up by teaspoonfuls and roll in confectioner's sugar.

Botamochi

Botamochi (also called *ohagi*), a sweet snack served on many festive occasions, is a favorite of all ages in Japan. Each little cake has a plain rice center covered with fudgelike brown *anko* (azuki/redbean jam).

Botamochi

Ingredients:

    1 cup red azuki beans

    1 cup sugar

    1 cup rice: mochi gome, American "sushi rice," or a 50/50 mix of these types. Do not use fluffy long-grain rice or instant rice.

Instructions:

NOTE: If you can buy redbean jam in a can (about 18 ounces), skip the first step. Instead, empty the can into a saucepan, stir and heat thoroughly, then let cool to room temperature.

1. First make the anko:

   Wash and rinse the beans, cover with water, and bring to a full boil for 1 minute. Turn off heat, cover, and let rest 1 hour.

   Drain the beans, rinse, and drain again. Add water to cover, plus ½ inch extra. Simmer gently, uncovered, until very soft, 30–50 minutes. (Or cook in pressure cooker according to manufacturer's directions 7 minutes; let cool naturally before opening.)

   Drain very thoroughly. Add sugar. Cook over medium heat, stirring constantly and mashing, until anko becomes almost as thick as mashed potatoes. Let cool to room temperature. This makes about 2 cups of traditional chunky anko. It can be prepared in advance and stored in the refrigerator, tightly covered. It thickens further as it cools.

2. Wash and drain the rice three times or until the water runs clear. Put rice and 1⅓ cups water in a heavy pan and cover. Bring to a boil, lower the heat, and simmer 15–20 minutes until rice is tender and water has been absorbed. Let rice rest, covered, 10 minutes.

3. Optional: You can "half kill" the cooked rice (see "Scary Snack" story) by mashing it in the pot with a potato masher or big wooden spoon.

4. Spread cooked rice in a shallow, nonmetal container to cool so you can handle it.

5. Using a square of plastic wrap or a sandwich bag and about ¼ cup cooked rice, firmly press the rice together to squeeze out air. Then press it into the traditional egglike oval shape. Repeat. Set the rice balls on a platter.

6. Spread about ¼ cup anko on the plastic wrap. Put a rice ball onto the anko, close the plastic, and gently press the anko until it completely surrounds the rice.

7. Open the plastic and gently tip the botamochi onto a serving dish. Repeat with remaining rice balls. Makes about 8.

Botamochi is traditionally served at room temperature on a small plate, eaten with chopsticks or a dessert fork. If many people are participating, each can shape one rice ball in a sandwich bag, add anko, and eat his or her snack from the sandwich bag.

Kappa Sushi Rolls

Sushi means "vinegared rice." There are many different shapes, toppings, and fillings. Some are rolled up in a sheet of *nori* (seaweed).

Sushi masters study for years to safely prepare sushi topped with *sashimi* (raw fish or seafood). Beginners shouldn't try it at home. But kappa rolls are a safe vegetarian version. Tradition says that kappas love cucumbers.

Kappa Sushi Rolls

Ingredients:

1 cup raw oriental-style short grain "sushi" rice (Do not use long grain or instant rice.)

3 tbsp rice vinegar

1 tbsp sugar

½ tsp salt

1 cucumber

wasabi (Japanese horseradish) paste

3 sheets of nori (dried seaweed), cut crossways in half: 6 pieces

makisu (bamboo mat for shaping sushi rolls)

Instructions:

1. Rinse and drain the rice 3 times before putting rice and 1¼ cup water in a heavy pan; cover. Bring to a boil, lower heat, and simmer until barely tender, 10–15 minutes (or use an electric rice cooker). Let it rest, covered, about 10 minutes. Sushi rice should be firm, not soft.

2. While the rice is cooling, combine the vinegar, sugar, and salt and heat, stirring until dissolved.

3. Spread the hot rice on a large platter or nonstick cookie sheet with sides. Sprinkle rice with the vinegar mixture while tossing and spreading the rice with a rubber spatula. When thoroughly mixed, spread rice out thin to cool so you can handle it. Traditionally, someone helps by fanning the rice. One cup raw rice makes about 2 cups cooked rice.

4. Peel the cucumber, leaving narrow stripes of green. Cut it in half lengthwise; scoop out and discard seeds. Cut the cucumber lengthwise in strips about ½ inch wide.

5. Place the bamboo mat on the work surface with ribs running crossways. Lay a half sheet of nori across it, rough side up. Spread $\frac{1}{3}$ cup rice over the nori, leaving a $\frac{1}{2}$-inch uncovered margin on the end nearest you, and a $\frac{3}{4}$-inch margin on the far end. Press and smooth the rice with *wet* fingers.

6. Press a strip of cucumber across the rice. Spread wasabi on it to taste. Brush a little water on the far margin of nori.

7. Lift the edge of the mat nearest you with both hands and use it to roll the rice/nori layer over the cucumber filling, pressing gently as you go. Don't catch the mat in the roll! The moistened end of the nori will seal the roll shut at the end. Using the mat, press and firm the roll into a cylindrical shape. Kappa rolls should be slim, about 1 inch diameter.

8. Set the completed roll on a cutting board. Cover with plastic wrap or a damp tea towel while you prepare the remaining rolls.

9. Trim off any cucumber sticking out the ends of the roll. Cut each roll into 6 pieces using a very sharp knife wiped with a damp cloth to keep the rice from sticking. Slice gently to preserve the roundness of the rolls. Set the slices on a platter, cut side up.

10. Serve kappa roll slices at room temperature. People can dip them in individual small dishes of soy sauce. Toasted sesame seeds are also good. Red pickled ginger makes a pretty and tasty garnish. Makes 36 bite-sized pieces.

NOTE: Using this method, you can also make rolls filled with a lightly steamed asparagus spear, or a row of green beans, or carrot strips, or raw avocado slices. If you want more than one filling per roll, it will need to be fatter; use a whole sheet of nori and $\frac{2}{3}$ cup vinegared rice per roll. This version makes 3 fat rolls, which can be cut into 18 pieces.

Home Style Miso Soup

You can make this quick soup as a light appetizer or a hearty main dish by varying the amount of vegetables. Experiment with combinations of vegetables and amounts of miso. Every family's favorite combination is different; a new bride struggles to serve her husband "soup like Mama used to make."

If you put *myoga* in it ("Plant of Forgetfulness"), use only enough for flavor.

Home Style Miso Soup

Ingredients for each serving:

1 cup water

¼ tsp *dashi no moto* (instant broth powder)

¼ cup (or more) raw vegetables (*quick-cooking:* green beans, snow peas, bok choy, cabbage, mushrooms; *slow-cooking:* carrot, potato, turnip, daikon, broccoli)

1 tbsp white or red miso

Optional: cubes of firm tofu, bite-sized pieces of cooked meat or seafood

Optional: 1 tsp *mirin* (sweet cooking wine) or sherry

Instructions:

1. Cut quick-cooking vegetables into bite-sized pieces. Cut slow-cooking ones in Julienne slices or matchstick strips so that they will get done at the same time. Hint: Buy prepared raw vegetables from a salad bar or the supermarket.

2. Bring water to a boil in saucepan. Add dashi no moto and vegetables. Simmer until the vegetables are just tender. Optional: Add the tofu, meat, seafood, or mirin.

3. Put the miso in a small dish, add a few tablespoons of broth from the pot, mash/stir the miso into this broth, then stir ⅔ of the mixture into the soup. Taste. If the flavor seems weak, add the rest of the miso. Do not boil the soup after adding miso.

4. Serve hot. Optional garnish: shreds of green onion or nori.

Japanese Green Tea

The secret of making good green tea is to brew it gently. Unlike black tea or herbal teas, the flavor is not improved by long steeping. The finer the quality of the tea, the cooler the water and the shorter the steeping time. You can even get a second round of tea from the same leaves by adding more hot water.

Freshly brewed green tea is traditionally served in small cups with no handles, which feel very good when you wrap cold fingers around them. But in summer, it is delicious cold.

Japanese Green Tea

Ingredients for each serving:

> 5 oz. water brought just to the boil
>
> scant tsp green tea leaves or 1 teabag

Instructions:

1. If using loose tea leaves, put them in a tea ball or use a teapot with a mesh strainer. Pour the water over the tea, steep just 1 or 2 minutes, then pour the tea into cups or remove the teabag/ball.
2. Do not add milk or sugar. Some youngsters may prefer it with a little honey.

Green Tea Ice Cream

Green tea flavor is so popular in Japan that it appears in all sorts of snacks, sweets, noodles, and even toothpaste. Green tea ice cream is very refreshing in hot weather.

Green Tea Ice Cream

Ingredients:

> ¼ tsp *macha* (powdered green tea)
>
> ½ cup sugar
>
> 2 cups milk
>
> ½ tsp vanilla

Instructions:

1. Stir macha into the dry sugar, mashing all lumps. Add a little milk. The tea powder resists getting wet! Gradually add the remaining milk. Stir in vanilla.

2. Freeze this mixture in an ice cream maker according to directions OR pour it about 1 inch deep into a metal or plastic bowl, cover with foil or plastic wrap, and put in a regular freezer until about half solid. Break up the chunks, mash and beat into slush, then cover and freeze again. The more times you repeat the mashing, the smoother the ice cream will be. Four servings.

Shopping List

anko: Redbean jam made from azuki beans and sugar. Canned anko comes as *koshi an* (smooth) or *tsubu an* (chunky).

azuki (*Vigna angularis*): Small red-brown beans with a sweet, nutty flavor, often available at health food stores. Sometimes spelled "adzuki" in English. Used in making anko and festive Red Rice.

dashi: Seafood-flavored broth, used as soup base and seasoning. Instant *dashi-no-moto* powder is comparable to instant bouillon granules.

macha: Powdered green tea used in tea ceremony and as flavoring.

miso: Thick paste fermented from ground soybeans, rice, and salt, used as soup base or seasoning, often available at health food stores. It has a salty, savory flavor. Soup is usually made from the "white" or "red" varieties; the stronger-flavored dark brown kind is used in sauces.

mochi gome: Sweet/glutinous rice, used to make mochi and rice crackers.

mochi ko: Sweet/glutinous rice flour.

myoga: Crisp buds of *Zingiber mioga,* a wild relative of ginger, with a flavor like ginger and garlic. Available seasonally in Asian grocery stores.

nori: Black seaweed in papery sheets for wrapping sushi or for garnishing other dishes.

tofu: Protein curd made from soy milk, comparable to fresh cheese curd. Available at health food stores and grocery store refrigerated produce cases. Use firm tofu in soup.

wasabi: Japanese horseradish paste, sold ready to use in tubes or as powder (prepare according to package instructions). Caution: It looks like mild guacamole but is very hot and spicy!

GAMES

Fox Exercises

This traditional hand game is fun and useful to fill odd moments in a program of stories. The first "exercises" are very easy for everyone, but the "ear twitch" is much trickier than it seems! Even adults find it challenging, which usually causes much surprised laughter. Be sure to practice in advance.

Note: Your spoken parts are in boldface print. Directions for your actions are in parentheses.

Here are two foxes. (Show how to make fox faces with your hands by pressing middle fingertips to thumb tip for the snout, raising the index and pinky fingers for the ears. See diagram A.)

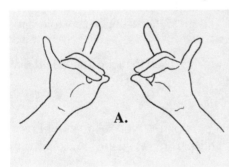

They need to exercise their necks.

First they look UP. (Tip your hands up at the wrist.)

Then they look DOWN. (Tip your hands down at the wrist.)

Up. Down. Up-down-up-down-up-down. (Repeat slowly until everyone is with you, then faster, as many times as they enjoy it.)

Next they exercise their necks to the LEFT. (Turn your hands to *your* right [the listeners' left].)

Then to the RIGHT. (Turn your hands to *your* left [the listeners' right].)

Left. Right. Left. Right. Left-right-left-right. (Repeat as above.)

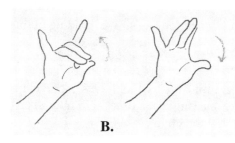

B.

Now they need to exercise their jaws. (See diagram B.)

They open their mouths BIG. (Open your fingertips wide; close.)

Then SMALL. (Open your fingertips just a bit; close.)

Big. Small. Big-small-big-small. (Repeat as above.)

Now it's time to exercise their ears. (See diagram C.)

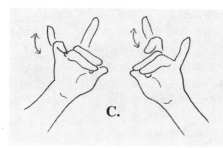

C.

First they twitch their LEFT EARS. (Bend just the end joints of *your* left index and right pinky fingers [the listeners' left].)

Then they twitch their RIGHT EARS. (Bend just the end joints of *your* right index and left pinky fingers [the listeners' right].)

Left. Right. Left-right-left-right. (Repeat as above.)

Whew!

One and One

This is a good game for uniting a restive group. It becomes happily loud, but winds down to quietness. Do it slowly at first, then speed up with a jazzy rhythm. They will probably want to repeat it! Note: Raising the correct number of fingers may be difficult for very young children, who may require extra time.

Note: Your spoken parts are in boldface print. Directions are in parentheses.

One! (Hold up both your index fingers, wave your hands to your left.)

And one! (Wave hands to your right.)

What (Wave hands left.) **kind of sound?** (Wave hands right.)

This (Wave hands down.) **kind of** (then up) **sound!** (Wave hands down/up.)

[*Tap, tap, tap*] (Tap your index fingers together three times.)

Two! And Two! (Repeat with actions as above, holding up index and middle fingers.)

(Increase stepwise to **Five! and Five!,** which gives a loud clapping sound. Then decrease one finger at a time, ending with just index fingers and whispering the chant.)

Rock, Paper, Scissors

The game we know as "Rock, Paper, Scissors" is called *Jan Ken Pon* in Japan. It is played very often by adults as well as by children. It decides not only which team starts with the ball or who is "it" in a game of hide-and-seek, but also who gets the last piece of candy or who has to carry the suitcase. In addition to the familiar hand version of the game, Japanese children play a very vigorous full-body version just for fun, using legs instead of fingers:

Two players face each other (Optional: join hands).

They chant together "Jan, Ken, Pon" (Optional: bounce in place on Jan and Ken).

On "Pon," each player jumps into one of the following positions:

Feet together = Rock

Feet apart = Paper

One foot forward, the other back = Scissors

As in the hand version, Paper covers Rock, Rock breaks Scissors, Scissors cut Paper. If both players take the same position, it's a draw. This version of the game is such fun that keeping score seems to be optional!

CRAFTS

Handkerchief Mouse

This mouse puppet can act out any of the mouse stories. Use a large cloth handkerchief or a cloth napkin (paper napkins and tissues are okay until the last step, when they usually rip).

Since exact measurements depend on the size of your cloth, please practice and experiment to see how far to fold up your edge, how far to cross the ends over, etc.

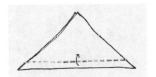

1. Fold cloth square in half diagonally to make a triangle.

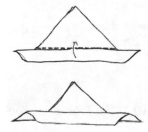

2. Fold up the bottom (long) edge twice.

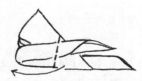

3. Turn it over (folds are now on the back). Bring left end across to right side.

4. Bring right end across to left side.

5. Fold top points down over the crossed ends.

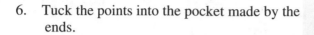

6. Tuck the points into the pocket made by the ends.

7. Rotate it so that the pocket is on top.

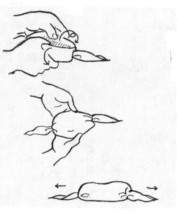

8. Put your thumbs in the pocket and gently fluff out this section to make a rounded body.

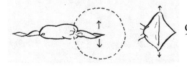

9. Unroll one end and spread the cloth sideways.

10. Fold the point under, making a small triangle.

11. Tie the triangle points in a knot.

12. The knot is the head; the points are the ears. The other end is the tail. It's a mouse!

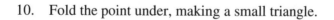

One-line Mouse

This is not a Japanese tradition but a simple design contrived by Fran Stallings for use with "The Mice Make a Pilgrimage" (part 1).

A.

Draw a sideways capital V, a figure 8, and a number 2 as in diagram A. When you draw them in one continuous line from the bottom edge of the V to the tail of the 2, they make a stylized mouse (see diagram B).

B.

C.

Add more mice, the nose (point of the V) of each new mouse touching the end of the previous mouse's tail, to make a chain of mice as in the story (see diagram C).

Kappa Toy

These toys were traditionally made from a length of hollow bamboo. Cardboard tubes are not as strong, but they are easier to get and much easier to work with.

> Cardboard tube 4½ inches or longer, 1½ inch or more in diameter
>
> 2 cardboard circles: trace and cut to fit the ends of your tube
>
> smooth, thick cord such as "rat tail" or sport shoelaces (Fuzzy yarn will not work.)
>
> Green paper, green felt (Kappas are usually green.)
>
> Craft glue
>
> Hole punch, pointed scissors, ruler, crochet hook or a hooked wire

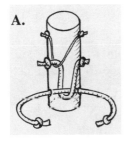

A.

1. Cover the tube and the cardboard circles with green paper. Let the glue dry.
2. Following diagram A for position and alignment, punch holes on opposite sides of the tube and at least half an inch from the top and bottom ends. Carefully use the point of closed scissors to poke holes halfway up the tube.

B.

3. Cut three cords. For a tube 1½ inches in diameter, cut 6 inches (middle = arms), 3 inches (top = ears), and 12 inches (bottom = legs). If your tube is wider than 1½ inches, you will need longer cords. At *one* end of each cord, tie a knot big enough so that it won't pull through the holes you punched. Leave the other end untied. Optional: if the untied end frays badly, stick the threads together with a little glue (see diagram B); let it dry before going on.

4. Use crochet hook or hooked wire to pull the untied end of the 6-inch cord through the middle set of holes. Tie a knot on the untied end.

5. Reach in the bottom of the tube with the hook and pull this middle cord down to the level of the bottom set of holes. Poke the hook in through one bottom hole, through the middle cord loop, out the other bottom hole; then, using the hook, pull the untied end of the 12-inch cord through the tube and loop. Tie off its end.

6. Pull on one knot of the middle cord so that it goes straight across. It will pull the bottom cord up into the tube, forming a loop inside.

7. Repeat step 5 at the *top* end of the tube, pulling the 3-inch cord through the tube and the loop of the middle cord; tie off its end. When you're finished, the cords will be connected inside the tube, as shown in diagram A. When you pull one cord straight through, the others become looped inside.

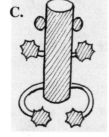

C.

8. From the felt, cut four each of ears, hands, and feet. Carefully untie one knot at a time and glue two felt pieces, like a sandwich, over the ends (see diagram C).

9. Glue the end circles in place (see diagram L, p. 157). Optional: Glue a paper fringe of "hair" around the top of the tube before putting the top circle on.

10. Decorate the kappa's face as shown in diagrams D and E.

When the glue is completely dry, you can practice pulling the kappa's weird limbs:

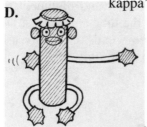

D.

First pull the middle cord back and forth (see diagram D) to show how his arms are connected to each other, as in the story "Kappa's Paper."

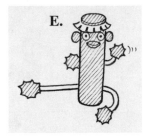

E.

Adjust the arms back to equal length. Now pull 1 foot (see diagram E). That leg will get amazingly longer as other the leg gets shorter—and the arms will disappear into the body!

Pull the legs back and forth to show that they're connected. Adjust the legs to equal length; now you can pull the arms out again—but both legs will get shorter!

Now pull one ear. It will pull way out from the head, while the arms get shorter!

Kappa Trick

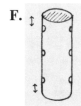

F.

You can also make a kappa trick by following directions 1 through 7 for the kappa but covering the tube and ends with any colorful paper and using three different colors of cord, each about 6 inches long (or more if your tube is wider than 1½ inches). (Diagram F shows the position of the holes the cord will be pulled through.)

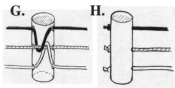

G.   H.

Construct the loops as for the kappa (diagrams A, p. 156, and G), putting large knots on one end of each cord so that it doesn't pull into the tube. It will look like diagram H.

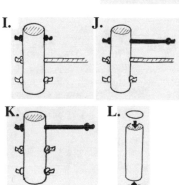

I.   J.

K.   L.

Pull the middle cord firmly to one side (top and bottom loops get pulled in). Tie off the top and bottom cords flush with the tube, cutting off excess cord (see diagram I). Then pull the top cord (pulling middle loop inside; see diagram J) and tie off the middle cord (see diagram K). Glue the end circles in place (see diagram L).

When the glue is completely dry, pull the middle cord out one side as far as it will go. The top and bottom cords should pull in so that only their knots remain outside.

Show people how the middle cord pulls freely back and forth. Then ask someone to pull one of the top knots. Of course the middle cord will disappear inside. Pretend to scold, "I said just pull the top one!" Pull the top cord back and forth showing what you "meant"; the middle one won't move further.

Then ask someone to pull "only the middle cord"; of course the top one will disappear inside. It works with the bottom cord as well. The results are so unexpected that people can't help laughing.

Can they guess how the cords are connected inside?

APPENDIX A: COMMENTS AND NOTES

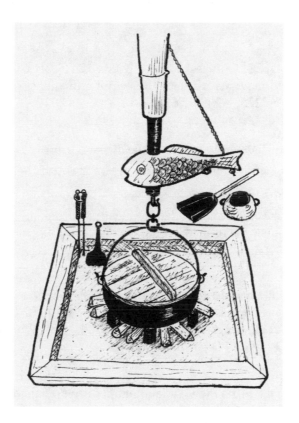

In this section, each story's title appears in boldface print followed by its number in Hiroko Fujita's *Katare Yamanba* collections (2.021 = volume 2, page 21) and its title in Japanese. Next comes Mrs. Fujita's oral or written COMMENT on the story and editor Fran Stallings's NOTE.

Following the comments or notes are scholarly citations based on Hiroko Ikeda's (1971) assignment of tale type and motif index numbers, and/or the classification numbers assigned by Fanny Hagin Mayer (1986).

Stories of Animals

Owl's Paint Shop 2.021 *Fukurou no Somemonoya*

NOTE: This story can become a participatory game in which listeners show off their knowledge of birds. Ask the listeners, "What kind of bird are you? What color do you want?"

"I'm Flamingo. I want to be pink!" "I'm Robin. I want a red vest and brown back."

When they become tired of this game or run out of ideas, you can proceed to Crow's part of the story.

Ikeda 249J "The Owl Dyer." Crow asked to be dyed (A2411.2.1.6). There are various explanations for why Owl made Crow black. Resentful crow attacks owl (A2494.13.1), so owl hides during day (A2275, A2491.2).

Mayer's variants 288 include crow or kite as the dyer.

Sparrow and Swallow *1.046 Suzume to Tsubame*

NOTE: *Shibui* in the swallow's song literally means "astringent, rough." But this same word can also mean "simple yet refined," and it is a high compliment for tasteful elegance in clothing or interior décor.

Ikeda 249A Sparrow and Swallow (or Woodpecker) were sisters (P252.1) News came that Buddha (or mother) was on deathbed (V212). Reward and punishment (A2220, 2230): sparrow can eat rice (A2435.4, Q65) but must hop (A2441.2.3). Vain (unfilial) bird (P236) complains she must eat dirt and bugs (A2426.2.12)

Mayer 268 The Sparrow's Filial Piety variant: mother is on deathbed.

The Tale of the Lizards' Tails 1.039 *Tokage no Shippo*

NOTE: There are several species of lizards that can indeed drop off their tails without bloodshed. The dropped tail wiggles for a while, distracting a hungry predator while the lizard escapes. Apparently it doesn't hurt, because the lizard soon resumes feeding or sunning itself. Eventually another tail-like extension can grow, but it has cartilage instead of bones.

Mayer 296 "The Lizard's Tail" doesn't mention God: Lizard just borrowed a human tail and thinks we have come to get it back.

The Fourth Leg 1.041 *Shihonome no Ashi*

COMMENT: Maybe some children will say, "There are some dogs which don't lift up a leg." Certainly female dogs don't. You had better be prepared with some response. Sometimes I return the question "Why is it?" to the children. Sometimes I say, "I wonder if the dog forgot that it came from God?" or, "I wonder if only male dogs had three legs?" or I promise, "I'll ask the dog next time."

Ikeda 200C A god /Buddha (V212) gave the fourth leg of a trivet to the dog, who carefully lifts that leg when he urinates (A2473.1).

Mouse Teeth 3.013, 6.020 *Nezumi-no Ha*

COMMENT: It's not the custom any more, but at the time when my baby teeth were coming out, we sang, "Exchange this tooth with a mouse tooth." We threw the tooth up to the roof if it was a lower tooth, and down into the space under the floor if it was an upper tooth. We wanted the new tooth to grow in as strong as mouse teeth.

There were many mice in the house where I lived in Fukushima. At night, I could hear them running around in the attic. It was as if they were having Sports Day every day. In the kitchen, in the closet, there were mouse holes. We tried to fight them by stuffing the holes with cedar leaves or nailing boards over the holes. But soon we found new holes right beside the stuffing. Mice really have strong teeth.

When you sing, "It was so tasty, last night's millet cake," I would like you to create a suitable melody. To make it sound like a children's song, you should emphasize the natural tones of speech and give it some rhythm.

Ikeda 2048 "The Weasel's Millet." Many versions begin with Weasel and Mouse agreeing to raise the millet crop together, but mouse claims to be sick (Type 9; K495) when the heavy work must be done. Then mouse steals the crop and eats with her children (K254, K364). Some versions have Weasel asking many animals (Z33) if they stole it. Mouse children accidentally reveal the theft (N450). Angry Weasel removes all but two pairs of teeth (A2345).

Mayer 324 "The Rice Field the Rat and Weasel Cultivated" begins with Type 9 as above. These versions don't seem to include a song (mouse children just beg for leftovers) or the ending where mouse steals the remaining millet too.

Earthworm and Snake 2.017 *Mimizu to Hebi*

COMMENT: When I tell this story, I sing like a European opera singer. People laugh and say it is not like a Japanese snake singing. But Takeda Kuni, the farmer who told me this story when I was small, sang it in that manner, so I believed that old Japanese snakes sang like opera singers.

Once I visited a nursery school and told this story to the children. The next day a teacher saw a child pressing his ear to the ground. Asked what he was doing, he replied that he was listening to Earthworm singing. The teacher asked him if he had heard it. He replied, "Yes, I did."

Those willing to hear it can hear it, I would say.

Ikeda 234 "Exchange of Eyes and Voice." The exchange is motifs A2332.6.4, A2421. Ikeda adds that the "song" of the earthworm is really made by a mole cricket.

Mayer 291 "When the Earthworm and the Snake Traded Eyes" includes a variant where Earthworm trades with Frog; but because Frog was greedy, the eyes were put on his back.

Sky Watcher 3.008 *Ten-maburi*

COMMENT: I have heard this story from many different people. Some used Otter and Monkey instead of Fox, and concluded that that's why monkeys have short tails. But I prefer Fox because I think the thick tail of a fox would attract more fish.

Ikeda 2K "Unjust Host." Fox pretends he must guard the sky (J1577) or ground (K1251.1.1). Otter, feeling cheated, tricks fox into fishing with his tail (Type 2; K1021). Some versions say trapped fox is killed by villagers or drowned by otter (J1565).

Mayer 318 "Tail Fishing" lists many variants featuring Fox and Otter. 319, "The Otter and the Monkey," is also a tail fishing story (without the sky-watching episode) explaining why Japanese Macaque monkeys have short tails.

Bracken and Snake 5.005 *Warabi to Hebi*

Mayer 293 "The Kindness of the Bracken" suggests that when people see a snake, they should ask it if it has forgotten the kindness of the bracken. One version claims that if you sing this song and spread bracken juice on your hands and feet, snakes will not bite you. Other versions say the pierced animal was a centipede or slug.

Melting Grass 2.046 *Torokashi kusa*

COMMENT: When I was a child, I just thought this was a scary story. I got more scared when I grew up and understood it fully. When we imitate others without understanding, we may fail.

In the old days snakes were all over, so there were many stories about snakes. They ate mice, which were a pest for our silkworms. Therefore, snakes were often called *Iegami-sama* (house guardian).

NOTE: In Japanese "*kusa*" (grass) means any non-woody plant, including what we would call "herbs," so we're not sure what kind of plant the snake ate. Mrs. Fujita says that Toshiko Endo also knew this story and once showed her the kind of "grass" it mentions, but they didn't test it.

This chilling story is useful in environmental education programs and other situations in which you want to make a point about the results of acting on incomplete or erroneous information.

Ikeda 612 "Snake Grass." Giant snake (B875.1) which has swallowed a man (F911.7) is seen by another man to consume a grass (B512; D965; D965.12) causing the body inside to be digested. Ikeda says this tale is popular with *rakugo* performers. She also heard that the tale type is common in China.

The Mice Make a Pilgrimage 1.023 *Nezumi no Ise Mairi*

COMMENT: This endless story is a test of the teller's skill and the listeners' patience. As long as everyone enjoys it, you can keep repeating, "Then the next dove in and bit the tail. Squeak squeak."

When I told this story in a kindergarten, I started to draw mice and connect them one by one until the blackboard was filled with them, but the children still kept saying, "Then the next dove in and bit the tail. Squeak squeak." I got the children to make handker-chief-mice and connect them one by one, saying, "Then the next one dove in and bit the tail. Squeak squeak." Ideas like this make these simple stories even more fun.

Ikeda 2300 "Endless Stories."

Stories of Village People

COMMENT: Doctors, officials, and priests . . . they are the people with power. Ordinary people had to put up with them in real life, so they made fun of them in stories.

When I was a child, I was often scolded, "Don't do that. People will laugh at you if you do that." "Being careful not to be laughed at" was a major theme of discipline at that time.

There were many stories about men with little brain. They were imaginary characters to be laughed at. We laughed at their mistakes. At the same time, we learned that we should-n't do such things. These days, we have lost that standard. Many young people today don't care what others think of them any more

NOTE: As explained in "A Brief History of Japan," the four traditional classes of non-noble people were samurai, farmers, artisans, and merchants. *Chojas* (rich men) played important roles in folktales but were not a separate class. A *shoya* (village headman) was appointed to lead the farmers, but mayors, magistrates, and provincial governors held the real power.

Table Manners *1.073 Imo Kororin* "Rolling potato"

COMMENT: The day after I told this story at a kindergarten, a child's mother said to me, "My child ate his dinner last night according to the manners he says he learned from you. How do you know the manners of *Ogasawara*?" [Ogasawara is one of the oldest, most high class styles of formal etiquette and culture, including the tea ceremony and flower arrangement. It goes back more than 1,000 years and was used in the emperor's court—editor.]

I heard this story from the farmer Takeda Kuni. It was handed down as a joke about ignorant farmers who don't know anything about manners. But it preserved the rules of old time etiquette. When I noticed this fact, I was surprised again at how great is the role of the old stories. Perhaps people in the old times taught manners with a story like this.

The government officers were not normally as friendly as this. Maybe this story was handed down wishing that there had been a magistrate like this.

NOTE: In the old days, farmers had to pay most of their rice crop to the government. It was called land tax. Farmers worked very hard to grow rice, but sometimes they could keep only enough for next year's seed. The farm families depended on noodles and dumplings made of wheat, barley, millet, or buckwheat. In bad years they might taste rice only as New Year's Day mochi. So rice was a treat for them.

When telling this story to American children, you might begin by saying that it will be "a story about underwear." Explain that until about a hundred years ago, men in most parts of the world wore loincloths instead of boxers or jockey shorts. Children may have seen pictures of sumo wrestlers wearing thick traditional loincloths.

It is fun to add audience participation to this story. You can invite the audience to try to remember Shoya's rapid instructions, to appreciate the difficulty of the sequence. When you reach the feast scene, invite volunteers to come onstage and play the roles of the farmers all-in-a-row. You are Shoya. Caution the row of volunteers not to act until the "farmer" on their right has acted, one step at a time. Typically they feel as relieved as the farmers when imitation keeps them safely on track—until the dropped sweet potato! Then they are glad to run offstage with their arms covering their heads.

Ikeda 1825D "Absurd Imitation." Leader, imitated by fools, drops food on the floor. They also imitate his warning gestures. J2498 (Type 1557), K2376. This episode in the "Village Fools Cycle" is told in Rakugo as "*Honzen*." Ikeda's collection includes many comic behaviors (cf. "the circulating slap") but apparently not the loss of underwear.

Plant of Forgetfulness 3.089 *Myoga-Yado*

COMMENT: The written word *myoga* consists of two Chinese characters. The first is the combination of "plant" and "name." The second is "burden."

NOTE: Myoga (*Zingiber mioga*) is a wild relative of ginger. The tastiest parts are the spring shoots and summer flower buds, which are picked just as they emerge from underground. Because of its strong flavor, like ginger with garlic, it is usually used as a condiment rather than as a vegetable dish.

Ikeda 1550 "Treacherous Inn-Keeper." Innkeepers feed myoga to rich traveler hoping he will forget his wallet (K2241) but he only forgets to pay them. Ikeda's collections do not include the sermon explaining why myoga is supposed to make one forgetful.

Mayer 240 also has only the innkeeper part of this story.

NOTE: Mrs. Fujita learned this story from the farmer next door when she was little. Later she found the sermon about Chu-ri-pan-taka in "Iguchi Stories" (Buddhist religious education for children), in which a priest under training told the origin of myoga. She has also found both the sermon and the innkeeper parts together in a Japanese dictionary of folktales.

Peach Peddler 4.101 *Momo uri*

COMMENT: In the old days, most marriages were arranged by the families. Sometimes the couple met for the first time on their wedding day. Although romantic love sometimes developed between them, it was not expected or considered essential for a successful marriage. Therefore, to traditional village people, a love match must have seemed strange and ripe for problems.

NOTE: "Tono-sama" means one's superior or master. It is not a specific name or rank, but a relative term used by anyone of lesser rank. This man was probably a hereditary regional ruler of the samurai class, who wore ceremonial swords but didn't fight as a warrior.

Ikeda 516B "Love Through Sight of Picture"

Farmer can't work because he wants to watch beautiful wife; she gives him her picture but wind carries it to castle yard (F962, N350). The lord falls in love with picture (H1381.3.1.2.1, T11.2), takes her from farmer (T481.5). She quits laughing or smiling (F591.2). Farmer comes to castle selling peaches/iris/new year pines/ chestnuts. Wife smiles at sound of his vending calls. Lord forces farmer to exchange clothes (K527.3), is locked out. They live happily in castle (L165).

Mayer 19

Mask of Oni 4.085 *Oni no men*

COMMENT: When I was a little child, I started first grade in Tokyo. But soon the war worsened and we had to leave Tokyo. First, I evacuated to Mitake with my grandmother and the youngest of my three elder brothers. The other two brothers and my parents stayed at our home in Tokyo. For that year until all of us were evacuated to Miharu Village in the mountains of Fukushima Prefecture, I was separated from my mother. Also during that year, my mother had a baby girl and I felt that the little sister deprived me of my mother.

So it was a very difficult year for me. I treasured the *otedama* (juggling balls) my mother had made for me. Once, one of the otedama got torn. I remember I felt very worried.

The *Otafuku* (happy woman) mask in this story is just an ordinary mask, but for the girl it is her emotional backbone. If something is wrong with it, she can't help being worried. I tell this story remembering my otedama.

NOTE: Papier-mâché masks such as Otafuku and Red Oni are sold at seasonal festivals. If you can get Otafuku and Red Oni masks, they add a lot to the telling of this story. You can wrap them in a *furoshiki* (Japanese carrying cloth) rather than the bulky wicker box mentioned in the story.

Ikeda 751C "Mask Mistaken for Face." Girl meets band of robbers (N765; cf. type 1676C), robbers mistake mask for demon and flee (J1793), leave money behind (N630). Her filial affection is rewarded by this treasure (Q22, Q65). In some locales this was told as a local legend.

Mayer 152

Doctor Who Dropped His Eye 5.057 *Mentama o Otoshita Isha-sama*

COMMENT: There is another silly story of a doctor. He took out, washed, and dried his eye, but a dog ate it up. So he used the dog's eye instead. After that, he couldn't stop smelling filthy things on the street, or sniffing around trash bins.

Ikeda 660D II "Horse-Chestnut Eyes." Man jumps down, eyes fall out, replaced backwards; he can see his own inside, becomes successful doctor (X372.) Ikeda's index also includes a version in which another man imitates the above actions but picks up horse chestnuts instead of eyes, becomes blind, must become a *zatobo* (blind professional storyteller) instead of a doctor (E781.1, J2415).

Boy with a Runny Nose 3.113 *Hanatare-Kozo-sama*

COMMENT: This is a story to teach us "Ask for more, and you will lose everything." But what I found interesting is a different part of the story. I have been involved in early childhood education for a long time. Children wipe their runny noses with their sleeves. Children play with their protruding navels. This story accepts such children as they are. By disliking and rejecting that, the old couple lost their magical good luck.

NOTE: Compare Aesop's "The Goose That Laid Golden Eggs" (D876).

Mayer 81

The God of Poverty 3.106 *Bimbo no Kami*

COMMENT: I heard this story from Toshiko Endo. We say we have hundreds of thousands of Shinto gods in Japan. They are a great match for Greek mythology. We have many gods inside our house, such as the god of the kitchen, the god of the cooking stove, and the god of the toilet. There are also many with whom we don't want to get acquainted, such as the god of poverty, the god of smallpox, the god of sickness, and the god of death.

In this story, the couple acquired happiness by taking care of a disliked god. There is some truth in this. That's why people kept telling these stories.

NOTE: Professor Harold Wright, when asked about whether "god" should be capitalized in these stories, replied, "When I was translating the Emperor Meiji's poetry and working closely with several Shinto Priests at the Meiji Shrine in Tokyo (one had studied in the school of religion at the University of Chicago) they insisted that I not use the capital 'G'. In fact they did not like the word 'god' at all. We agreed to use lower case 'deities' since the word *kami* usually indicates more than one. No capital at any rate."

Ikeda 735B "God of Poverty" takes a different turn. Discovering that god of poverty (F480) lives with them, poor and lazy couple decide to move but he comes along (F481.3, F482.3.1.1; N251.7) so they give up and go home. They start working hard; when they become wealthy, he becomes uncomfortable and leaves.

Two Strong Men 5.113 *Niou to Dokkoi*

COMMENT: It is true that in Japan, we say "Dokkoi." So it might be true that in China, they say "Niou." Or it might be untrue. I can't guarantee it.

Niou in folktales was a delinquent boy. He was strong and fooled around at night. Nobody could stop him. But one day a priest preached to him and he became a temple courtyard guard. Now he is watching at the temple gate.

Ikeda 1962A "The Great Wrestlers." Japan's champion wrestler (X940) named Niou goes to China to compete with Gaoo (H1225). Frightened when Gaoo's wife/mother easily lifts something he can't budge, he fears husband/son must be stronger still (J31). Flees in a boat, pursued with chain which he files off. Story explains origin of exclamations while lifting heavy objects, statue of Niou guarding temple gate.

Foolish Greetings 2.061 *Baka musuko no Aisatsu.*

NOTE: When I tell my version of "Lazy Jack" in Japan, Mrs. Fujita often introduces it by telling this story. The Japanese folktale "What Should I Have Done?" (Ikeda 1696B: gifts carried inappropriately, lost) is an even better parallel to Lazy Jack.

Ikeda 1696A "What Should I Have Said?" Foolish young man (I.121, Z253) acts inappropriately at a funeral (J2461.1.2.1; J2461.3). Parent says he should express sympathy (J2461;

J2461.2). He follows instructions literally at a wedding; fire; blacksmith; quarrel; fighting bulls (J2516; J2461.1.2; Z20).

Mayer 248 "The Son-in-Law's Oral Instructions." Trying to remember what to say, foolish young man blundered every time.

Tea-chestnut-persimmon-vinegar 2.054 *Cha-kuri-kaki-su*

NOTE: The challenge in telling this story is to say the calls in a single breath! It is fun for the audience to try calling along with you. Since the words in English are much longer than the Japanese, we recommend using the Japanese words—which will also sound more nonsensical to English speakers.

Mayer 243 "Tea-Chestnuts-Persimmons." Foolish store assistant ran words together, no one could understand. Told to say each word by itself, he called "vinegar is vinegar by itself," etc.—all run together.

Pickle Bath 2.067 *Deko-buro*

COMMENT: This is a very famous story in Fukushima, and everyone there knows it. The above version is for children. For adult audiences, I add the following: "The old woman, peeking into the bathhouse, said, 'I only brought one pickle. Why does he have two?' "

Ikeda 1262 "How the Fool Cools Hot Water." Foolish son-in-law (L121, Z253) visits in-laws, observes father-in law cooling his hot tea by stirring it with a slice of radish pickle. Finding his bath water too hot, he asks for a pickle and stirs with that (J2420).

Scary Snack 4.069 *Han Goroshi*

Ikeda 1339 "Ignorance of Rice Cakes." Foolish visiting son-in-law overhears pestering child being told that mochi is a ghost, don't come near it (J1732). Declines to eat it, carries package on long shoulder pole (J1782). When it slides down pole to his neck, he thinks it is attacking (J1495).

Mayer 251 "Rice Cakes Are Ghosts." Bride, afraid that foolish husband would eat too much while visiting her parents, warned him that "mochi" means "ghost." He did foolish things from fear of it.

Stories of Priests and Apprentices

Sutra of the Mouse 1.018 *Nezumi Kyo*

COMMENT: An oral storyteller can get away with repeating the young apprentice's mumble many times while the mouse continues to do different things. You can hold listeners' attention by varying the tone and accent of your voice. But when a story like this is recorded on paper, the eye becomes bored with the repetitions. So printed versions of this kind of story often omit many of the repetitions that are such fun in the oral telling.

NOTE: In Japan and elsewhere there are similar stories in which robbers misunderstand what they overhear and guiltily frighten themselves away. An American Appalachian version is "Old One Eye" (N611.2 criminal accidentally detected).

Ikeda 1530 A "Sacred Chants Inspired by the Action of Mice"

[Various situations] people beg to learn sacred chants (Type 910B; J163.4) The priest does not know Buddhist texts but pretends, inspired by actions of mice he sees (K1961). These nonsense words are chanted faithfully every night (J2495). Thief (thieves) plan(s) to break in but hear chanting, (is) are scared away because (his) their actions seem to be detected by person in the house (J2493, N611.4, Q20).

Mayer 205

The Floating Coffin 3.069 *Neko danka*

COMMENT: At my aunt's funeral, a priest chanted a sutra in a wonderful voice. He was so diligent that his chant went on and on. It was such a blessed thing, but listening to the long sutra without understanding a word was a kind of torture to me. My feet were numb from kneeling for a long time. Moving my hips, hoping nobody would notice, right to left, and then left to right, I hoped the sutra would end soon.

Then suddenly, familiar words jumped out from the sutra. "*Namu-kara-tanno, tora-nyah-nyah.*" I was surprised. I looked up, wondering if my aunt's cremation urn had risen into the air. My suffering was gone. I started to smile secretly at the repetition of this phrase, remembering the girl's coffin coming down little by little from high in the air.

Long ago when I learned the story, I was taught that the cat said "*tora-nyah-nyah*" ("tiger meow meow") because it had tigerlike stripes. What the funeral priest actually said was "*tora-yah-yah.*" Later I learned this phrase is a protection against evils, from a precious sutra called "*Daihi-enman-muge-sinjyu.*" Perhaps somebody made up this story while listening to this precious sutra, trying to pass the boring time.

Ikeda 215C "The Grateful Cat of a Mountain Temple." Poor priest advises cat to live elsewhere. Cat predicts (B560) that rich man's daughter's coffin will rise and stay in mid-air, advises poor priest to chant "Namu, Tora ya . . . ya." and cat will make coffin come down.

Other priests fail, poor priest succeeds. Rich man builds a new temple for him. Ikeda says, "This tale is sometimes told as a true story or local legend."

Mayer 129

A Debate in Sign Language 2.102 *Konnyaku Mondo*.

COMMENT: In Japan when people are misunderstanding each other but don't realize it and keep talking, the situation is called *"konnyaku mondo"* ("konnyaku conversation").

According to Buddhism, the earth is not a globe but a flat plane. So it seems strange that the monk asked "the earth?'" by encircling a globe. But I heard this story this way when I was a child, so I tell it this way, too.

Jodo (Pure Land, Paradise: the Ten Directions north, east, south, west, southeast, southwest, northeast, northwest, up, and down) is a very clean and holy place where a great number of spirits gather. In this story, the monk asked how our spirits can get there after death.

The Five Commandments are quite important for Buddhist believers. They are, "Do not murder, do not steal, do not commit adultery, do not tell lies, and do not drink." The monk thought that konnyaku-ya's five fingers meant that obeying these five commandments was the way to go to Jodo.

"Three Thousand Worlds" refers to all the worlds before life, during life, and after death, where avatars of Buddha have taught.

Ikeda 924 "Sign Language Misunderstood." A layman takes the place of mountain priest who fears he cannot win a dispute on Buddhist theories (K1961). Visitor and layman dispute in gestures; visitor admits defeat and leaves (N685). Visitor attributes profound meaning to layman/priest's gestures, but layman thought they were discussing his konnyaku (H607.1, H1804). The story is sometimes performed by rakugo. Versions are known in China and Korea.

Fu Fu Pata Pata 2.085 *Fu Fu Pata Pata*

Ikeda 1541 "Miser Tricked into Sharing Food." After sending acolytes to bed, priest eats mochi cakes alone (W152.12). Acolytes ask to have their names changed to words which sound like blowing, etc. (K2310); when priest blows on cakes that night, Fufu pretends he was summoned and priest must share (J1341, K362.1).

Mayer 183 d

New House Mochi 2.088 *Tatemae-no Mochi*

COMMENT: It's hard to tell how many pillars you should construct. But as long as listeners are enjoying the story, you can make up as many as you want.

Ikeda 1567A "The Hungry Acolyte." Stingy priest sends acolyte to check on new house, so that he can eat mochi cakes alone (W152.12). Acolyte knows this, returns early and uses poker to draw floor plan in ashes, discovering the cakes (J1341, J1344, J1500). The priest has to share with him.

Mayer 183 e

How Much Rice? 5.117 *Yubi aizu*

COMMENT: I've heard similar stories about a family entertaining guests. In one story, the head of the family decides whether to offer dinner to the guest or not and sends signs by his cigarette smoke. In another story, he decides which rank of sushi they should order for the guest and tells it with the number of his coughs.

Ikeda 1567B "Cooking Agreement." Priest instructs acolyte to cook one sho of rice for one finger, two for two etc. (H607). When priest falls into outhouse, raising both hands, acolyte cooks ten sho of rice (J1341, W152.12).

Stories of Strange Happenings

A Poet's Ghost 4.092 *Utayomi no shi*

COMMENT: It is said that one who dies without any regrets, having completed what he needed to do, can go straight to heaven. But you cannot go to heaven easily if you die without completing your task, or leave your little infant behind, or without satisfying your grudge, and so on. Probably those people can't accept their deaths.

At a funeral, the priest addresses the last instructions to the soul through Buddha's words: "You died, and you are going to heaven. Do you understand?" Even with this advice, some still have regrets in life, and they become ghosts.

The poet in this story couldn't go to heaven because he died without completing his poem. When you tell this story, it will be entertaining if you chant the poem in a ghostly voice after the poet became a ghost.

It is getting harder to tell this story because few people nowadays have experience with open hearths. We only see them in pictures, at museums, and in historical dramas on television. Even fewer people know that *oki* is a chunk of wood that is glowing red, as well as a view of the ocean horizon.

NOTE: The finished poem is:

Kakimazuru
Hai-wa Hamabe-no
Suna-ni-nite
Irori-wa Umi-yo
Oki-ga Miyuru-ni

Ikeda 326H "The Ghost of a Poet Laid to Rest." Fearless poet/priest appeases a poet's ghost (H1411) by completing his unfinished poem. Ghost never reappears (E451.10). A similar tale is told in Okinawa as a local legend. Elsewhere the emphasis is on the pun in the poem.

Spirits of Old Things 3.054 *Furu gasa furu mino furu chiyochin*

COMMENT: When I was growing up, I was taught the following process. Worn out *yukatas* (cotton kimono for summer) became sleepwear. The worn out sleepwear was made into diapers. The old diapers became rags. After that, I was supposed to chant "Nanmaida" and throw the rag into the outhouse pit to decay. Later it fertilized the farm field and I suppose it went up to heaven.

Times have changed. But we should still make full use of things so that they won't become goblins and haunt our homes. It is painful for them not to be used or fixed.

Ikeda 326B "Old Abandoned Utensils Haunt a Temple"

You Are Watched 4.032 *Nerawarete iru*

COMMENT: This is a very scary story. You might be someone's target without knowing it.

A proverb says, "Correct your conduct by observing that of others." Perhaps we can't see ourselves from outside, but by observing others, we can reflect on ourselves. If you speak ill of someone, someone will do the same to you. If you are mean to someone, someone will be mean to you.

Cf. Ikeda 2076 "Chain of Absentmindedness." Husband doesn't realize his pipe is empty, wife watching him sews up the sleeve of kimono she is making, maid watching them dishes rice onto floor instead of bowl, manservant watching all three neglects to make heel on straw sandal, makes it three feet long. (Z20 cumulative tales.)

The Home of the Bush Warbler 4.120 *Uguisu no Sato*

NOTE: Although Japan now follows the Western solar calendar of twelve months, the traditional year had thirteen lunar months. Festival dates, now fitted into the solar calendar, don't always match the agricultural seasons they originally celebrated.

Uguisu (*Cettia diphone*) is a small, shy, green and brown bird that is usually visible only before the trees leaf out. Its distinctive mating call, heard throughout much of Japan from the start of spring, is loved as a sign of springtime. The beauty of its song led to the English name "Japanese nightingale," but the Japanese bush warbler does not sing at night, so this name is no longer commonly used.

Ikeda 480E "Efficacy of bird's prayer"

Mayer 131 Farmer hired as estate caretaker. Single forbidden room contains all the merits (*hokekyou* = Sutra of the Lotus) she had been collecting for many years. When he opened the forbidden door, they flew away.

Snow Woman 2.122 *Yuki Joro*

COMMENT: Even today, we sometimes read in papers that some people freeze to death, losing their sense of direction in the snow. It even happens in their own neighborhoods.

If you are standing alone in the snow, you can easily imagine the falling snow being a woman's shadow, and the blowing wind being a baby's cry.

Snow covers everything in white. It makes the world around us different, fantastic. That's why we have so many stories about snow.

Ikeda 768A "Child Becomes Heavier While Being Held." At night, a strong hero (F610) meets a young woman holding a baby by a bridge/ford/graveyard (E425.1.4). She asks him to hold the baby while she is gone awhile. Baby gets heavier and heavier (D1687; G303.3.5.3). (These other versions apparently do not mention snow.)

Mayer 332

Stories of Yamanbas

Mr. Sun's Chain 1.123 *Tentou-san no Kusari Nawa*

COMMENT: The part where Yamanba sweetens her voice and smoothes her hands to deceive the children is similar to "The Wolf and Seven Kids," collected by Grimm, but indeed a mother sometimes makes victims of her children. A mother who spanks children "for their own good," a mother who confines her children feeling that "they can't do anything without me," and a mother who kills her child along with herself because she "can't bear leaving the child behind" is a yamanba. Like this, a mother controls her children as she wants. "Every mother is a yamanba" is my personal opinion.

But fortunately when they grew up a little, children find ways to escape from their mothers. In this story, the two older children ran away from the situation.

Ikeda 333A "Gluttonous Ogress and Children." Ogress (Q11.3), having eaten the mother, goes to house disguised as mother to eat the children. Suspicious children notice that her hand is rough; she smoothes it (K1839.1). They notice her hoarse voice; she drinks oil/sugar/honey (F556.1.1, K1832) and is admitted. Ogress eats the baby (K2011). Children hear munching and ask for food; she gives them baby's finger (G86). Insisting they need to visit outhouse, children are let out and climb a tall tree (R251). Ogress follows their false instructions (K619.2) and falls. Children call to upper world for a strong rope, ascend (F51), become stars (A761, R321). Ogress imitates, gets rotten rope (X111.7), falls to ground (K963) and her blood stains roots of millet.

A Wife Who Doesn't Eat 2.112 *Kuwazu Nyobo*

COMMENT: In the old days, brides' lips were painted in a tiny bow shape, much smaller than their natural size. Perhaps it suggested that the women were not big eaters or chatterboxes. But they were just pretending because men wanted them to be so.

Men who grew up with the old teaching that the sexes should be segregated from each other after the age of seven tended to misunderstand women. Some of them seemed to dream that feminine women just lived on air.

NOTE: Mugwort (*Artemisia vulgaris*) is a very useful plant with a strong aromatic scent. Added to mochi, it makes tasty healthful *kusa-mochi*. Crumpled mugwort stops the bleeding of wounds. The fine soft hair from the underside of mugwort leaves is also used in traditional oriental medicine for moxibustion to relieve the pain of gout, arthritis, etc.

The leaves of sweet-flag (*Acorus calamus*) resemble the sword-shaped leaves of iris ("blue flag") but have a sweet, spicy scent. They were used to perfume water for hot tubs and washing hair. The plant was also a symbol of samurai bravery.

Ikeda 1373A "The Wife Who Does Not Eat" Man wishes for wife who does not eat (N699.6), marries apparently ideal woman but becomes suspicious. When he spies on her from the ceiling (W153.2.1) he discovers that a mouth on her head consumes huge quantities of rice. She agrees to divorce but asks for the bath tub (J1545.4). He escapes through irises and mugworts, still celebrated on May 5 (A1540).

Mayer 107, 108

Clothes Bleached in the Moonlight 2.118 *Tsuki no Yozarashi*

COMMENT: In the old days the villagers labeled independent women as too selfish. There were other kinds of sad women, too: pregnant women who were not married, divorced women who were rejected by their own families . . . . I think Yamanba was there to support these women.

This is a scary story. This woman is not impulsive. She spends several months in preparation, during which her husband never notices her plan. She is young and beautiful, not a Yamanba with wild white hair. When she finishes sewing her husband's kimono, she quite naturally helps him wear it—with the right side over the left. It means death. I demonstrate it as I tell. All these touches make this story very scary.

I'm more interested in the "old woman of the mountain." Did she do the same thing as this woman when she was young? That might be the reason she is living away from the village. What she does for this young woman is abetting murder. But she is too strong to worry about it. In this story, nothing is told about this old woman. That makes me wonder more about her. Is she Yamanba?

This old woman of the mountains could see a man's real nature, which didn't show on the outside. It often happens that men who are regarded as philanthropists in society are extremely stingy when they are with their families, or a man who is seen as amiable and kind by society is domineering toward his wife and children. It is possible that even if all the others say that he is a good man, his wife cannot stand to live together with him as husband and wife.

This old woman had probably had similar experiences in the past herself. Not only her own experiences but also the wisdom that she had accumulated over many years may have made her take action to help this girl.

NOTE: Six Way Crossroad: The Six Ways represent the worlds of delusion, the opposite of *Jodo* (Pure Land/Paradise; see notes for "Debate in Sign Language"). Six Way Crossroad means the crossroads of the dead, so old-time villagers gave this name to the crossroads at the edge of town, or the crossroads that lead to a cemetery. In folktales, scary things often happen there.

The god of night rules over the spirits of the dead.

Ikeda 365 "Clothes Made by Moonlight." Only daughter of rich man develops extreme dislike of husband, asks old woman sorceress (N825.3) what to do. The moment husband puts on the clothes she has made following full moon instructions, he exits and is never seen again (D1792, M430). Old woman advises how to learn what happed to him. Waiting at crossroads under full moon, wife sees dead husband (D2061.2.4); he passes as if floating and whispers poem (A487).

Picking Mountain Pears 2.126 *Yamanashi-Mogi*

COMMENT: The old woman who taught the brothers how to get to the mountain pears was probably Yamanba. The first two brothers failed because they didn't listen to her. My understanding of this story is that Yamanba taught the importance of listening to nature. One of my friends, who is quite a mountain climber, once said to me, "You won't meet an accident if you listen to nature. But it is very difficult to obey nature." I feel this story tells the same thing.

Traditional country people listened to the sounds of nature while working. For example, they would begin planting rice when the locusts began to sing in early summer. They would mend their clothes and prepare for winter when they heard crickets. Such a way of living must be reflected in this story. You should listen to nature and when nature is rejecting you, you should never rush, even more so if you are in a hurry. I like to think that the third son had a heart that listened to the sounds of nature and a spirit that waited patiently, and it was that composure that led him to success.

Ikeda 551 "The Sons on a Quest." Three brothers seek marvelous pears (D981, H1324, H333.3.2) to cure their parent. They meet old woman who predicts what will happen, gives advice (H971.1, N825.3). Two older brothers are impolite to her (Q2), ignore signals of water-fall (D1311.3), rustling bamboo, chirping birds (B143.1). Youngest follows instructions (B122.1, H991, H1242), succeeds (L10). Monster tricks elder brothers (C730). Youngest kills monsters and restores brothers (E64).

Old Woman's Skin 5.146 *Uba kawa*

COMMENT: I think this Basama is really a Yamanba because the skin disguise works through magic. Yamanba often helps women in distress. [See notes for "Clothes Bleached in Moonlight"—editor.]

This tale is similar to "The Princess with a Bowl over Her Head," in which the dying mother puts a bowl over her daughter's head and tells her not to take it off. This bowl protects the girl until she meets the man of her life, and provides supplies that support her. The mothers' maternal warmth protected and supported their daughters even after they had grown up and out of their care.

When I heard this story from Toshiko Endo, it took two hours. She explained in great detail how the stepmother was hard on the girl. In the old days, women learned tips for their work through listening to this kind of story. Mrs. Endo said that if the wife is clever, the family will prosper, but even a good husband can't prosper if he has a foolish or lazy wife!

There are stepchild stories all over the world. They all have the same conclusion: the stepchild who was ill treated ends up happier than the stepmother's spoiled child. It might be a message from our ancestors that we should not spoil our children, that if we are hard on them, they will become happier in the end.

But you can't just be hard on children. In stories, there is always some thing, human, spirit, or animal, to protect the stepchild. In this story, it's Basama. A child needs strictness on one side, and support on the other, in order to grow fully.

NOTE: Compare this story with worldwide Cinderella variants. "The Girl and the Geese" is an Egyptian folktale in which a "witch" gives a young woman an old woman's skin to use as disguise. She gets a job with a rich family, whose son sees her in her true form while she is bathing and becomes lovesick for her. (*Folk Tales of Egypt* retold by Denys Johnson-Davies, Cairo Egypt: Hoopoe Books, 1993. ISBN 977-5325-14-5.)

Ikeda 510B "Magic Skin." Persecuted heroine abandoned by orders of stepmother (S31; L55). She is given a magic skin (K512) which can turn her into an old woman (D530, D1025,K521.1). Disguised (K1815), she is hired by rich household (L131) where youngest son accidentally sees her without disguise (H151.6.1), becomes love-sick (T24.1). All the female servants try offering him tea etc. (cf. H315) but when he sees heroine he recovers (H111). After marriage, all family brides are tested (H375) but she wins.

Stories of Supernatural Creatures

NOTE: Although Tanuki and Kappa stories are important in Japanese folklore, Ikeda and Mayer indexed only a few, and most of them do not match Mrs. Fujita's tales exactly. Some tales about Fox are elsewhere told about Tanuki! We picked the most representative examples for this book.

Tanuki (*Nyctereutes procyonoides*) is an Asian animal belonging to the dog family. I think it looks like a slender fox wearing a thick raccoon coat. In the folktales, Tanuki characters are almost always male. They love to drink sake and pound on their potbellies, especially under a full moon.

The Moon Sticks Out Its Tongue 4.012 *Shita o dashita Tsuki*

COMMENT: People believed a Tanuki would climb up a tall pine tree and change his feet into clouds. The more clouds he wanted, the more feet he needed for them, and if he wanted four clouds he would naturally fall down.

Ikeda 66B "Hidden Fox Betrays Self." People trick the shape-changer into revealing his true nature.

Spooky Tanuki Music 6.058 *Kaidan jitate no tanuki-bayashi*

NOTE: In some variants, there is a contest to see who can bang the loudest. The foolish Tanuki beat their bellies until they burst! Dead Tanuki are found on the ground next morning.

Tanuki Who Turned into a Die 6.064 *Saikoro Tanuki*

The Fox Barber 2.078 *Kamisori Gitsune*

Ikeda 145B "The Boaster's Head Shaven." I. Man boasts he can't be bewitched by a fox (J2351.1.1; N455; W117), sees a fox transform into a young matron holding a baby (D313.1). II. The people of the house do not believe him. III. He tries to reveal the fox by force but woman/baby dies. Priest offers to take him as disciple. IV. Priest shaving his head with dull razor is really a fox, they are all foxes.

Mayer's 193 is like Ikeda parts I & II.

Fox Teakettle 5.010 *Kitsune no chagama*

COMMENT: The song is about my home town Miharu (three spring times), where plum trees, peach trees, and cherry trees bloom at the same time, bringing three springtimes at once.

Ikeda 325 "Trick Sale of the Fox." Grateful fox (B360, 366) transforms itself (D610) into a tea kettle (D420) and has itself sold, profiting (D612, K252) its benefactor. Variants of this tale type are very popular and widespread in Japan, sometimes featuring Tanuki instead of Fox (D1171.3.1). Several temples claim it happened there.

Mayer 122

A Hoin Monk and a Fox 3.023 *Hoinsama to Kitsune*

COMMENT: When children beg me to tell them a scary story, I often tell this one. If older children are enjoying the suspense, I repeat the climbing pursuit many times.

A traditional Buddhist funeral procession is called *Nobe-okuri*, but I know some old people who call it *Jaran-pon*. This is because in the old days, people walked to the cemetery making those sounds with drum and cymbal. I have attended this kind of funeral only once. It was very unusual and impressive. For example, we wore straw sandals to the cemetery and left them there. We took a different route home, wearing the street shoes we had carried.

NOTE: To help young listeners understand that the shape-changer Fox is responsible for Hoin's visions, use the Japanese hand sign for "fox" (see "Fox Exercises" in part 7) both in the opening scene and again at the end where Fox laughs.

Ikeda 612C "The Coffin Bursts: Dead Arises." Yamabushi priest tricks sleeping fox with blast of horn, fox falls into stream (see also 612B, 612D). It becomes dark (D908, D2146.2.1, F965, K1889.5). A funeral procession approaches; priest climbs tree to avoid meeting it; they abandon the coffin. The corpse appears from the coffin (E261.2.1) and pursues priest up the tree until he falls into the stream. This was a trick of the fox (B857).

Mayer 194 gives only the first part of the story, no funeral or corpse.

Kappa's Paper 5.033 *Kappa no shoumon*

NOTE: In Fukushima they tell of a nasty kappa who lurked in the toilet pit of an outhouse, bothering ladies who used the facility. An old granny stopped this by cutting off his hand and keeping it. To get it back, Kappa not only promised to cease mischief but also gave her some of the magic ointment with which he had reattached his hand. She became a famous healer.

Ikeda 47C "The Water Monster Dragged by a Horse." Kappa tries to pull a horse under water but is dragged to the farmer's house instead. Kappa writes an affidavit promising not to do mischief anymore; such a document is sometimes treasured by local families.

A Kappa and a Fish Peddler 5.036 *Kappa to Isabaya*

NOTE: Stories of *ongaeshi* (repayment of a debt of honor) are found throughout Japanese folklore: A crane, cat, turtle, or other rescued animal insists on repaying a human's kindness.

Ikeda 47C Kappa's Life Spared (K1022.2.1). The monster in gratitude brings fish to the house every night (B370, B584).

APPENDIX B: GUIDE TO WORDS IN THIS BOOK

Pronunciation Guide

Japanese pronunciation is very clear, and no sounds are skipped over. Every consonant + vowel syllable gets its own equal beat. Doubled consonants and extra vowels each get their own beat. Even *-n*, the only single consonant, gets a beat in songs and poetry. The vowel sounds are similar to Italian or Spanish:

a as in "father"

e as in "pet"

i as in "ski"

o as in "so"

u as in "rhubarb"

Glossary

In these lists, each word is in boldface type. Japanese words are in boldface italics, followed by their pronunciation, showing stressed syllables with capital letters. If a word is in all lowercase letters, please try to say the entire word flat. Literal translations appear in parentheses. The English definition follows the colon.

Baka Musuko ba ka mu su KO: foolish son, the protagonist of many silly stories that teach by bad example

Basama BA sa ma: old woman, granny

betsubetsu BE tsu be tsu: separate, distinct

botamochi bo ta MO chi: sweet snack: ball of half-pounded rice covered with brown azuki bean jam (see recipe section in part 7)

Buddha: the Enlightened One, founder of Buddhism

butterbur: plant with large rhubarb-like leaves; as with rhubarb, only the stalk is eaten

chiyochin chi YO chi n: paper lantern

cho CHO (a pair): even numbers (2, 4, 6, etc.)

choja CHO ja: rich man, self-made millionaire

daikon DA i ko n: very large, long, white radish served pickled (*takuan*), or cooked like turnip, or grated in sauces

furu FU ru: old, worn-out

futon FU to n: Japanese bed, a mattress and thick quilts spread on the floor

geta GE ta: wooden clogs

Ise I se: site of nationally important Shinto shrines

Hai! HA i!: "Yes, I heard you" (does not necessarily mean "I agree")

han HA n (half): odd numbers (1, 3, 5, etc.)

han-goroshi ha n GO ro shi (half killed): alternate name for *botamochi*

hibachi hi BA chi: small charcoal brazier

kaki KA ki: persimmon

kasa KA sa: umbrella made of oiled paper and bamboo

kimono ki MO no: clothing; long robe wrapped and tied with a sash

koban KO ba n: large oval gold coin, very valuable

konnyaku ko n NYA ku: tofu-like gel, important in vegetarian diets

Konnyaku-ya ko n NYA ku ya: person who makes and sells konnyaku

koto KO to: large stringed instrument

kuri KU ri: chestnut

kusare nawa ku sa re NA wa: rotten straw rope

kusari nawa ku sa ri NA wa (iron rope): chain

mina-goroshi mi na GO ro shi (all killed): alternate name for mochi, because rice is all pounded into smooth dough

mino MI no: traditional raincoat made of layers of straw

miso MI so: savory thick paste made by fermenting soybeans with bran and salt, used as soup-base and seasoning

mochi MO chi: snacks made of smooth-pounded rice (see recipe section in part 7)

mon MO n: small coin, worth only a little

mugwort: common wormwood (*Artemesia vulgaris*), an aromatic herb used in folk medicine or as seasoning

Mukashi mukashi, aru tokoro ni mu KA shi mu ka shi, A ru to ko ro ni ("Long long ago, in a certain place") : traditional beginning of a Japanese folktale

myoga MYO ga (plant from a man carrying his name): strong-flavored vegetable that tastes like ginger and garlic (*Zingiber mioga*)

obaasan o BA a san: grandmother

oki O ki: open sea; glowing embers

oni O ni: ogre, devil

Oshimai! o shi MA i ("The end!") :
traditional ending of a Japanese
folktale

Otafuku o TA fu ku: smiling woman
portrayed in masks and folk art

rowan: mountain ash tree (*Sorbus
aucuparia*)

sake SA ke: alcoholic beverage distilled
from fermented rice or other grains

Sakyamuni sa kya mu ni: one of the
incarnations of Buddha

-sama -SA ma: very honorific suffix
added to a name, comparable to
"Sir/Ma'am"

samurai SA mu ra i: warrior class in old
Japan

-san -SA n: polite suffix added to a name,
comparable to "Mr./Mrs./Ms."

shibui shi bu I: bitter, nasty, rough. Also
simple yet refined, elegant

Shinto SHI n to (The Way of the Gods):
ancient religion of Japan, with
thousands of deities

shoya SHO ya: village headman, leader of
the farmers

somen SO me n: very thin noodles, a
summertime favorite

su su: rice vinegar

sumo SU mo: Japanese wrestling

sutra: Buddhist scripture

tabi TA bi: socks with a separate big toe,
worn with thong sandals

Tanabata ta na BA ta: Star Festival (July
7), celebrating the Milky Way

tanuki TA nu ki: Asian canine
(*Nyctereutes procyonoides*),
sometimes translated "raccoon dog"
or (very misleadingly) "badger";
tanuki is tanuki.

tatami ta TA mi: resilient floor mats,
covered with woven straw

teuchi te u chi (kill with sword): alternate
name for udon noodles

Tono-sama TO no sa ma: not a name, but
a respectful term used by people of
each rank for the rank above them

tora TO ra: tiger

udon U do n: wheat noodles made of
rolled dough cut into long strips,
similar to linguini pasta

waraj wa RA ji: straw sandals

yamanba ya MA n ba (old woman of the
mountain): "witch" or "ogress" (But
see the introduction to part 5.)

Zen: form of Buddhism seeking
enlightenment through self-discipline
and meditation, rather than through
study of scripture

Chants

Momo, momo, momo iran ka na?
moMO, moMO, moMO i-RAN ka
NA? ("Peaches, peaches, don't you
want [to buy] some peaches?")

Namu amida butsu NA mu a mi da but su
(Hail, Amida Buddha): most basic
Buddhist sutra

Nanmaida NA n MA i da: The drone
when people don't know their
prayers or are mumbling

Sound Effects

Try to pronounce these nonsense syllables so that they imitate the intended sound.

amu, amu: munch munch

becha, pita, pita: human body percussion

bo chan!: big splash

bo, bo, bo: fire

Bu bu: "oink, oink"

chika chika: sunshine

choro choro chorori: scampering

do-don: water falling

Fu! Fu!: "Huff! Puff!"

garigari: crunching

gatagata: rattling

giko, giko: file scraping back and forth

gokun: swallowing

Guenko!: "Yip!" (fox kit crying)

Hon-gyaa!!: "Wah!" (infant crying)

jara-jara-bon: rattling dice

jori: scrape of a dull razor

jyaran, pon, chin: drums and chimes of a funeral procession

kappora: stirring

koro koro koro: rolling; or scampering

koto koto, kon, kon: stirring and cooking

Kyu kyu kyu (earthworm song): high-pitched singing

mosora, mosora: scuttling

musha, musha: chewing

Niau, niau: "meow meow"

non non: softly falling snow

Nyah-nyah: "meow meow"

pata pata: hopping or brushing

pero pero: flickering tongue

po-n, poko, poko: tanuki body percussion

poTOn!: plop!

saara-sara: wind rustling the leaves

shanari, shanari: lady's kimono swishing as she walks

ston: boom; crash

suru suru suru: slithering down; or fast climbing up

ton ten, teke-teke: rhythms beaten on drum's face and rim

ton-ton: chirping

Wan wan: "bow, wow"

zaza zaza: pouring rice

zunga, zunga: trudging along

zuru zuru, nyoro nyoro: slithering snake

zuru zuru zuru: slow climbing

Types of Japanese Storytellers

Note: The first three were once professional guilds but have died out in modern times.

Biwa Hoshi bi wa ho SHI: blind male, traveling solo; head shaved like a priest; recited ancient epics and histories accompanied by *biwa* (Japanese lute)

Zatobo ZA to bo: blind male, traveling solo; played *shamisen* (Japanese banjo) and told a variety of story types

Goze go ze: blind female tellers traveling in troupes of two or three with a partially sighted leader; played *shamisen*

Rakugo-ka ra ku GO ka: male comic stage entertainer for adults; kneels on a cushion, using fan and towel as versatile props. The *rakugo* (witty monologue) usually has a surprise ending, unexpected plot twist, or pun. Rakugo-ka can sometimes be seen on Japanese television.

Kamishibai ka mi shi BA i (paper drama): candy sellers who gathered a crowd of children by reading a story off the backs of illustrated cards stacked in a frame, often mounted on a bicycle

Kataribe ka TA ri be: traditional tellers of local folktales, orally learned, often in heavily accented and archaic language (corresponding to the late American traditional teller Ray Hicks)

New Katarite ka ta RI te: modern (revivalist) volunteer tellers or professional educators/librarians who tell stories learned from books as part of their work in schools, libraries, and *bunko* (private neighborhood libraries for children)

Ohanashi obasan o ha NA shi O ba san (auntie storyteller): lively traditional or revivalist teller who works with children; children sometimes call Mrs Fujita "Ohanashi obaasan" (granny storyteller) while adults often call her Kataribe.

BIBLIOGRAPHY

Sources

Fujita, Hiroko. *Katare Yamanba*. Vols. 1–6. Tokyo: "The Young Yamanbas," 1996, 1997, 1998, 2000, 2003, 2004.

    Hiroko Fujita's followers recorded and transcribed the colloquial Japanese folktales she told, with her commentary. A seventh volume was published in 2006.

Ikeda, Hiroko. *A Type and Motif Index of Japanese Folk-literature.* FF (Folklore Fellows) Communications No. 209. Helsinki: Suomalainen Tiedeakatemia, Academia Scientiarum Fennica, 1971.

    Ikeda categorized and summarized (in English) the tales collected by Japanese folklorists, assigning tale-type numbers and Aarne-Thompson motif index numbers.

Mayer, Fanny Hagin, trans. and ed. *The Yanagita Kunio Guide to the Japanese Folk Tale.* Bloomington: Indiana University Press, 1986.

    Mayer translated Yanagita Kunio's scholarly analysis *Nihon mukashibanashi meii* (1948), providing the tales in synopsis form with Kunio's detailed notes about local variants. *Note:* These classification numbers follow a different system from Aarne-Thompson, and they do not match the numbers assigned by other Japanese folklorists.

References

Algarin, Joanne P. *Japanese Folk Literature: A Core Collection and Reference Guide.* New York: R.R. Bowker, 1982.

    Algarin surveyed Japanese folktales available in English.

Endo, Toshiko. *Endo Toshiko no katari* (*The Telling of Toshiko Endo*). Transcribed and edited by Hiroko Fujita. Tokyo: Isseisha Publishing, 1995.

    Fujita preserved 200 folktales in colloquial Japanese from the repertoire of a Fukushima elder. Unfortunately this rich resource is not yet available in English.

Lanham, Betty B., and Masao Shimura. "Folktales Commonly Told American and Japanese Children: Ethical Themes of Omission and Commission." *The Journal of American Folklore* 80, no. 315 (January–March 1967): 33–48.

> Authors asked which folktales Japanese parents were still telling their children in the 1960s.

Mayer, Fanny Hagin, trans. *Ancient Tales in Modern Japan: An Anthology of Japanese Folk Tales.* Bloomington: Indiana University Press, 1984.

> Mayer provides full retellings of representative tales in English.

Recommended Reading

Kawai, Hayao. *The Japanese Psyche: Major Motifs in the Fairy Tales of Japan.* Translated by Gerow Reese. Dallas, TX: Spring Publications, [1988] 1996.

> Kawai analyzes major folktale themes from a psychological point of view, particularly focusing on male and female roles.

Kazuko, Emi, and Yasuko Fukuoka. *Japanese Cooking: The Traditions, Techniques, Ingredients and Recipes.* London: Anness Publishing, 2001, 2003.

> Detailed explanations of ingredients and methods for preparing traditional and modern dishes.

Recipes

The Rice Cooker's Companion: Japanese American Food and Stories. San Francisco: National Japanese American Historical Society, , 2000. http://www.njahs.org.

> Stories of the Japanese American immigrant experience, including World War II internment camps, family life, and customs, especially in Hawaii and California. The recipes range from solidly traditional to very Americanized adaptations.

See also the many excellent, beautifully illustrated books on Japanese cooking that are now available. The photos are essential because Japanese people value beautiful arrangement of the food almost as much as its taste.

Crafts and Games

Fujita, Hiroko, and Fran Stallings, ed. *Stories to Play With: Kids' Tales Told with Puppets, Paper, Toys, and Imagination.* Little Rock, AR: August House Publishers, 1999.

> Stallings translated and adapted for Americans the first of Fujita's how-to handbooks for Japanese storytellers (including four Western stories learned from Stallings). Each story has directions for making simple props and crafts, which encourage beginning tellers. Additional handbooks, published in Japanese by Isseisha Publishing Company, await translation.

Readily Available Japanese Folktales

English-language picture books and collections of Japanese folktales have tended to focus on a subset of popular stories. While these are indeed widely known and beloved in Japan, they reflect only a fraction of the Japanese folk repertoire.

Individual books seem to go out of print rapidly, but you can find many of the following popular stories in your library or through interlibrary loan.

Boy who drew cats
Fox/Badger tea-kettle
Gratitude of crane/stork wife/daughter
Issun boshi (Little One Inch)
Izanagi & Izanami creation myth
Jellyfish seeks monkey's liver
Kaguya-hime (Shining Bamboo Princess)
Kintaro/Golden Boy
Magic Listening Cap
Magic Mortar/Salt Mill
Magic straw cape of invisibility
Mirror of Matsuyama
Momotaro (Peach Boy)
Mouse seeks a husband
My lord bag of rice
Old man who lost his wen/hump
Old man who made cherry trees bloom
Princess who wore a bowl on her head
Robe of feathers
Roly-poly rice ball/Funny little woman
Shipei Taro
Tanabata (Milky Way; weaving maid and herd boy)
Tengu's magic fan
Terrible leak
Tongue-cut sparrow
Urashima Taro
Uri hime (Melon Princess)
White hare of Inaba

INDEX

ABOUT THE EDITOR AND CONTRIBUTORS

Fran Stallings is a professional storyteller and writer living in Bartlesville, Oklahoma. She met Hiroko Fujita in 1993 and has managed annual American storytelling tours for her since 1995, also working with Mrs. Fujita in Japan and Singapore. Stallings edited and adapted one of Mrs. Fujita's Japanese handbooks on storytelling, published in the United States as *Stories to Play With* (August House, 1999). Her publications include articles, stories, songs, and three CDs. Her academic training in biology informs her environmental work as "EarthTeller."

In 2003 Fujita and Stallings received the National (U.S.) Storytelling Network's International StoryBridge Award for their work on both sides of the Pacific. They hope that this book will make Mrs. Fujita's stories available to English-speaking story lovers everywhere.

Hiroko Fujita was born in Tokyo in 1937. During World War II her father evacuated the family to the rural mountain town of Miharu in Fukushima Prefecture. They knew no one there; he just liked the town's name, which means "Three Spring Times."

Like the children in C. S. Lewis's *The Lion, the Witch, and the Wardrobe,* young Hiroko discovered magic in this wartime retreat, but it was the magic of ancient folktales. She heard most of them from Mr. Takeda Kuni, a farmer who worked the field next to her family's two-room cabin. She also heard some tales from elders in her family and in the households of school friends. Later, as a young woman in Fukushima City, she heard additional tales from Mrs. Toshiko Endo, an elder who had also grown up in rural Fukushima Prefecture.

Mrs. Fujita graduated from Tokyo Women's University and for more than forty years has been involved in early childhood education. Now she visits kindergartens, nursery schools, libraries, local health centers, and community centers throughout Japan, handing down nursery songs and games to young mothers. She also lectures and writes on parenting. She has written over two dozen books in Japanese. She lives in Kashiwa, Chiba Prefecture, Japan.

Although she is at home on a festival stage or in a classroom full of children, Mrs. Fujita does not consider herself a "pro-teller" but rather "*ohanashi obaasan*" (storytelling granny) in the traditional folk style. Storytelling for her is a part of everyday life.

Kyoko Kobayashi, illustrator, was born in Ibaraki Prefecture in 1957. She is a self-taught artist and has illustrated many of Hiroko Fujita's books published in Japan as well as *Stories to Play With*. She now lives in Matsudo-city, Chiba Prefecture, with her husband and her three children. Recently she started taking Quigong lessons to get away from her busy everyday life for a while.

Harold Wright, emeritus professor of Japanese language, literature, and culture at Antioch College, is an award-winning translator of Japanese poetry. His books include translations of and commentary on Japanese literature from the eighth through the twentieth centuries. His honors include fellowships from the Ford Foundation, Fulbright, the National Endowment for the Arts, Endowment for the Humanities; the Japan Foundation, and the Translation Center Award.

With his wife, Jonatha, he is active as a storyteller and performance poet. Their work takes them often to Japan, where they collect and research Japanese stories, often in the oral tradition. They have taught storytelling classes at Antioch and other colleges.

Miki Sakurai, founder and current president of Japan Storytellers Association, performs at festivals and many other occasions in Japan and other countries. Using the notion that a storyteller is a story-creator, Miki retells folktales, writes, publishes, and lectures in order to cultivate other storytellers.

Makiko Ishibashi (major translator of the tales, and interpreter/liaison with Japanese contributors) grew up in Matsuyama-city, Ehime-prefecture, and went to the University of Tokyo. She lived in St. Louis for several years while her husband did postdoctoral work and their two sons attended American schools. Upon returning to Japan she taught private English classes for children. She loves gardening and playing piano.

Recent Titles in the
World Folklore Series

Mayan Folktales; Cuentos Folklricos Mayas
Retold and Edited by Susank Conklin Thompson, Keith Thompson, and
*   Lidia López de López*

The Flower of Paradise and Other Armenian Tales
Translated and Retold by Bonnie C. Marshall; Edited and with a Foreword
*   by Virginia Tashjian*

The Magic Lotus Lantern and Other Tales from the Han Chinese
Haiwang Yuan

Brazilian Folktales
Livia de Almeida and Ana Portella; Edited by Margaret Read MacDonald

The Seven Swabians, and Other German Folktales
Anna Altmann

English Folktales
Edited by Dan Keding and Amy Douglas

The Snow Maiden and Other Russian Tales
Translated and Retold by Bonnie C. Marshall, Edited by Alla V. Kulagina

From the Winds of Manguito: Cuban Folktales in English and Spanish (Desde
los vientos de Manguito: Cuentos folklóricos de Cuba, en inglés y español)
Retold by Elvia Perez, Edited by Margaret Read MacDonald

Tales from the Taiwanese
Retold by Gary Marvin Davison

Indonesian Folktales
Retold by Murti Bunanta, Edited by Margaret Read MacDonald

Folktales from Greece: A Treasury of Delights
Retold by Soula Mitakidou, Anthony L. Manna with Melpomeni Kanatsouli

Gadi Mirrabooka: Australian Aboriginal Tales from the Dreaming
Retold by Pauline E. McLeod, Francis Firebrace Jones, and June E. Barker;
*   Edited by Helen F. McKay*

Additional titles in this series can be found at www.lu.com